History of Mexico

1000 Interesting Facts from Ancient Times to the Present

© **Copyright 2023 - All rights reserved.**

The content contained within this book may not be reproduced, duplicated, or transmitted without direct written permission from the author or the publisher.

Under no circumstances will any blame or legal responsibility be held against the publisher, or author, for any damages, reparation, or monetary loss due to the information contained within this book, either directly or indirectly.

Legal Notice:

This book is copyright protected. It is only for personal use. You cannot amend, distribute, sell, use, quote, or paraphrase any part, or the content within this book, without the consent of the author or publisher.

Disclaimer Notice:

Please note the information contained within this document is for educational and entertainment purposes only. All effort has been executed to present accurate, up-to-date, reliable, and complete information. No warranties of any kind are declared or implied. Readers acknowledge that the author is not engaging in the rendering of legal, financial, medical, or professional advice. The content within this book has been derived from various sources. Please consult a licensed professional before attempting any techniques outlined in this book.

By reading this document, the reader agrees that under no circumstances is the author responsible for any losses, direct or indirect, that are incurred as a result of the use of the information contained within this document, including, but not limited to, errors, omissions, or inaccuracies.

Welcome Aboard, Check Out This Limited-Time Free Bonus!

Ahoy, reader! Welcome to the Ahoy Publications family, and thanks for snagging a copy of this book! Since you've chosen to join us on this journey, we'd like to offer you something special.

Check out the link below for a FREE e-book filled with delightful facts about American History.

But that's not all - you'll also have access to our exclusive email list with even more free e-books and insider knowledge. Well, what are ye waiting for? Visit the link below to join and set sail toward exciting adventures in American History.

To access your limited-time free bonus, go to: ahoypublications.com/

Table of Contents

Introduction 4
Pre-Columbian Mexico (14,000 BCE–1519 CE) 5
Conquest and Colonization of Mexico by the Spanish (1519–1821) 8
Chichimeca War (1550–1590) 11
Mexican War of Independence (1810–1821) 14
First Mexican Empire (1822–1823) 17
First Republic of Mexico (1824–1835) 20
Texas War of Independence (1835–1836) 23
The Centralist Mexican Republic (1835–1846) 26
Caste War of Yucatán (1847–1901) 29
Mexican-American War (1846–1848) 31
The Reform War (1858–1861) 35
The Second Mexican Empire (1864–1867) 39
Expansion of Industrialization (1890–1940) 41
The Mexican Revolution (1910–1920) 44
The Cristero War (1926–1929) 48
Institutional Revolutionary Party Era (1929–2000) 50
Mexican Oil Expropriation (1938) 53
Bracero Program (1942–1964) 56
Student Movement of 1968 60
Mexican Debt Crisis (1982–1988) 63
Cultural Revitalization Movement (1980–Present) 66
Mexico City Earthquake (1985) 69
North American Free Trade Agreement (NAFTA) (1994) 72
Formation of the Party of the Democratic Revolution (PRD) (1989) 75
Zapatista Uprising (1994) 78
Migration to the United States (1970s–present) 80
National Action Party (PAN) Era (2000–2012) 83
Election of Andrés Manuel López Obrador (AMLO) (2018) 85
War on Drugs (2006–present) 88
Increase in Gang Violence (2010–present) 91
Sports in Mexico 94
Mexican Actors, Musicians, and Celebrities 97
Conclusion 100
Sources and Additional References 101

Introduction

Mexico is a nation with a captivating history, culture, and people. It is a nation that has seen a plethora of revolutions. **This book offers an extensive exploration of the vast and tumultuous timeline of Mexico's past**, from the days of grand **pre-Columbian civilizations** to the aftermath of the 2018 election of **Andrés Manuel López Obrador.**

Beginning with the first known inhabitants in 14,000 BCE, readers will be taken on a journey through the **pre-Columbian era** and its **indigenous societies**, **the Spanish conquest** and colonization of Mexico, **the formation of Mexico's first empires**, and the impact of wars, such as **the Mexican-American War, the Reform War, and the Cristero War. Additionally**, this book will investigate the industrialization and cultural revitalization movements and the significance of **Andrés Manuel López Obrador's** election in 2018. His influence on **modern-day Mexicans** is vast, and you'll be surprised to learn the many ways he has brought—and keeps bringing—his country to the world stage.

Who hasn't heard of Mexico's white beaches and resorts that dot its coast? Or mariachi bands and savory dishes? On the darker side, **Mexico battles** the violence of drug wars led by powerful cartels and has suffered from a great migration of people.

Throughout **this book**, readers will gain an understanding of **the many forces that have shaped Mexico's rich culture** and **how the people of Mexico** have been resilient in the face of oppression and hardship. Gain insight into **the complex relationship between Mexico and the United States**, including **the Bracero Program, NAFTA**, and **the migration of Mexicans to the United States.**

By the end of this book, **readers will have insight into how the nation developed and an understanding of the Mexican people's creativity and resourcefulness** that have allowed them to build a strong and diverse nation. With this knowledge, readers will be well equipped to better explore the fascinating history **of this extraordinary nation**.

Pre-Columbian Mexico
(14,000 BCE–1519 CE)

For centuries, the ancient people of Mexico have captivated us with their unique culture, beliefs, and practices. From hunting and gathering to exchanging goods to playing board games like **patolli, the ancient Mexicans** have left a lasting legacy. In this chapter, we will explore the enthralling history of **the ancient Mexicans** and their remarkable accomplishments in art, science, engineering, and more.

1. **Ancient people in Mexico used stones to make tools and weapons** to help them hunt and gather food.
2. **For centuries, the people of Mexico used a system of trading** that didn't involve money. Instead, they exchanged goods like food, tools, clothing, and even cocoa beans!
3. **The ancient people of Mexico built homes out of mud bricks.**
4. Ancient Mexicans **played a game called patolli**. It was a board game that involved betting. People would bet trade goods, but sometimes, they would bet their property and even their family!
5. **Ancient Mexicans believed in many different gods and goddesses** and held ceremonies to honor them.

6. **Ancient Mexicans made very accurate readings of the sun, moon, and stars.**
7. **Ancient Mexicans were masters at engineering,** building networks of canals to help with irrigation.
8. The ancient **Mexicans were known for their skill in weaving intricate patterns into their clothing** and blankets.

9. **Ancient Mexicans wrote many of their stories and beliefs on stone tablets** and buildings.

History of Mexico

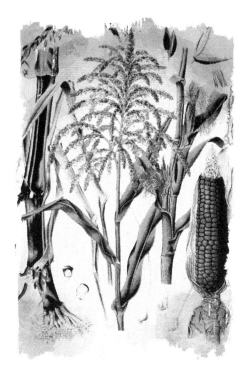

10. **Ancient Mexicans were experts at growing and harvesting corn**, which was an important part of their diet.
11. **The ancient Mexicans used cocoa beans to make a bitter drink called xocolatl.**
12. **Ancient Mexicans traded in gold, silver, and turquoise jewelry,** which were symbols of status and wealth.
13. **Ancient Mexicans created colorful artworks from clay and stone.** Many of these artworks tell stories of their gods, goddesses, and heroes.
14. **Ancient Mexicans kept birds, turkeys, and dogs** as pets and for food.
15. **Ancient Mexicans created colorful masks and costumes to use in their ceremonies and festivals**, which is one reason colorful feathers were so valued.

16. **Ancient Mexicans celebrated the solstice** with special ceremonies and feasts.
17. **Ancient Mexicans built pyramids and temples** to honor their gods and goddesses. These pyramids are generally much different than those found in Egypt.
18. **Ancient Mexicans had a complex system of writing** that used pictures to represent different words and ideas.

19. **Ancient Mexicans believed that their ancestors could communicate with them** from the afterlife.
20. **Ancient Mexicans played musical instruments like drums, flutes,** and rattles to make music.
21. **Ancient Mexicans held competitions to decide who was the best at skills like running and ball playing,** with one game similar to basketball.
22. **Ancient Mexicans made colorful decorations from feathers, shells, and beads.**

23. **Ancient Mexicans**, like many people around the world, **had shamans** or what people used to call medicine men or women. These people studied the natural world for plants and other things to help in healing. They also served as a conduit between the sick and injured and the gods.

24. **Ancient Mexicans used a calendar that was based on the seasons,** the sun, and the stars.

25. **Ancient Mexicans believed that their gods and goddesses** could be found in every part of nature.

26. **Ancient Mexicans practiced religious sacrifices** by offering up valuable items like gold, food, or even people to the gods.

27. **Ancient Mexicans believed in the power of dreams** and used them to try and make sense of the future.

28. **The chief god of the Aztecs was Huitzilopochtli.** He was considered the god of the sun, war, and human sacrifice. Human sacrifices were offered to **Huitzilopochtli** to ensure his favor and protection.

29. **Ancient Mexicans built cities and trading centers** that grew to become some of the largest in the world.

30. **Ancient Mexicans built long, straight roads** to help them travel from one place to another.

History of Mexico

Conquest and Colonization of Mexico by the Spanish
(1519–1821)

In 1492, Christopher Columbus became the first European to land in the Western Hemisphere since the Vikings. His voyage was made on behalf of **the Spanish monarchs Ferdinand II and Isabella I.** The men who followed him in the next few years were called **conquistadors** ("those who conquer"). A group of **conquistadors arrived in Mexico in 1519** with one goal in mind: establishing a Spanish empire in the new and untamed land. **The Spanish brought horses, gunpowder, a new religion, technologies, and weapons with them**. **Mexico was transformed by the Spanish,** who built new cities, roads, and bridges and established a new system of government. It is a testament to **the Spanish conquistadors'** ambition, power, and tenacity that their legacy remains in Mexico to this day.

31. Born in Medellín, Spain, in 1485, **Hernán Cortés became the leader of the Spanish conquest of the Aztec Empire.**

32. **Cortés played a significant role in the introduction of Christianity to the Americas.** He brought Catholic priests with him and established churches and monasteries throughout the newly conquered territories.

33. **The Spanish were looking to increase their trading opportunities.** However, they often seized territory and people rather than trading with the locals fairly.

34. **Spain was looking to expand its empire and gain access to new resources, such as gold and silver**, when it decided to colonize Mexico in 1519. Adding new territory would also give Spain additional power and prestige.

35. **Horses, a key component of the Spaniards' success, were introduced to Mexico by Cortés's army.**

8

36. **The Spanish used weapons the Aztecs had never seen before**, such as early pistols, muskets, and cannons.

37. **The Aztecs were no match for the small Spanish force of five hundred people** with their new weapons.

38. **The Spanish also practiced the policy of "divide and conquer,"** promising people who had been subject to Aztec rule more power and wealth if they helped the conquistadors. Disease also took a toll on the Aztecs and other native people.

39. **Over the next few decades, the Spanish began to colonize lands to the north and south of Mexico,** including Florida and Central America.
40. **Roman Catholicism was brought to Mexico by the Spanish.** Many native people of Mexico were forced to convert to Christianity or face death.
41. **The Spanish began to force the Aztecs and many other tribes in Mexico to learn their language.**

42. **The Spanish replaced the Aztec legal system with their own**, though both included the death penalty and other harsh penalties.

43. **The Spanish established a new taxation system in Mexico** based on the encomienda system, which meant farmers had to give a share of their crops to the Spanish.

44. **A new currency, the peso, was introduced to Mexico by the Spanish.** It was also known as "piece of eight," which is a popular term in pirate and treasure-hunting stories.

45. **The Spanish established the first universities in Mexico.**

46. **The Spanish established a new system of education in Mexico** that largely consisted of religious teaching and information about the glory of Spain and its kings and queens.

47. **The Spanish brought new forms of medicine to Mexico,** such as the cinchona tree, which was later found to contain quinine, to treat malaria. The Spanish had conquered parts of South America, and many of the people there used the plant for a variety of medical reasons.

History of Mexico

48. **Cows, pigs, and potatoes, essential ingredients for a successful agricultural society, were introduced to Mexico by the Spanish.**

49. Even before the Spanish arrived, **the Aztecs had already developed sophisticated irrigation systems.**

50. **Many of the conquistadors were only concerned with gaining wealth,** and many searched throughout much of Mexico for El Dorado, a legendary city made of gold. Other Spanish expeditions in South America and Florida had the same goal.

51. **Baroque and Neoclassical styles of architecture**, as well as new forms of art, including painting, sculpture, and music, **were brought to Mexico by the Spanish.**

52. **New forms of literature, such as the novel and the epic poem, were introduced to Mexico by the Spanish.**

53. **Technologies, such as the printing press and the compass, were brought to Mexico by the Spanish.**

54. **Many new roads and bridges were built by Spain** to connect the cities of Mexico.

55. **The Spanish built many new cities in Mexico, including the capital, Mexico City. The great Aztec city of Tenochtitlan** had stood there since around 1325.

56. **The population of Tenochtitlan before the Spanish was about 250,000.** After the Spanish conquest, the number of native people in the area declined because of diseases brought by the Spanish.

57. **The Spanish brought diseases like smallpox to the New World**. The natives had no built-up immunity to those diseases. Millions of people died as a result.

58. **The conquistadors established the first European settlements in Mexico, including Veracruz and Mexico City. Mexico City, originally known as Tenochtitlan**, was built on the ruins of the Aztec capital.

59. **A large number of African slaves were brought to Mexico by the conquistadors,** as were natives from Cuba, another territory the Spanish had colonized.

60. **The Spanish discovered new crops in the New World, such as tobacco, cocoa, bananas, pineapples, and more**.

Chichimeca War
(1550–1590)

> **The Chichimeca War is a pivotal yet often forgotten chapter in Mexico's history.** For nearly a century, this devastating conflict brought **Spanish colonialism** to the front door of **the Chichimeca people**. Despite their valiant efforts, **the Chichimeca were eventually defeated in 1590.** The war also marked the beginning of **the Spanish colonization of all of Mexico,** which the Spanish called **New Spain.**

61. **The Chichimeca War** (1550–1590) was a series of conflicts between **the Spanish Empire and the indigenous Chichimeca people** of central northern Mexico.

62. **The Chichimeca War was one of the longest and bloodiest wars in New Spain's history.**

63. **The Chichimeca War was a major conflict between the Spanish and the indigenous people in Mexico.** The war lasted for decades and cost the lives of tens of thousands of people.

64. **The Chichimeca weren't a tribe but a confederation of the Pames, Zacatecos, Guamares, Guachichiles, Caxcanes, Otomí, and Tecuexes.** They were all semi-nomadic hunter-gatherers who lived in the north-central region of modern-day Mexico.

65. **The Chichimeca War began when the Spanish began to make incursions into the Chichimeca territory in search of silver and gold.**

66. **The Spanish also committed widespread sexual assault on Chichimeca women,** which is what spurred the tribes to fight.

67. **The Chichimeca people fought fiercely against the Spanish by utilizing guerrilla tactics.**

68. **The Spanish used a combination of military force and missionary activity** to subdue the Chichimeca people.

69. **The Chichimeca people were known as fierce warriors and were known to use a variety of weapons,** especially bows and arrows.

History of Mexico

70. **Chichimeca arrows were made from reeds with an obsidian head that was sharper than a razor blade.** This arrowhead could pierce Spanish armor!

71. **The Chichimeca were also renowned for their use of guerrilla tactics**, such as ambushes and raids, that often threatened Spanish food supplies.

72. **The Spanish responded to the Chichimeca guerrilla tactics by forming large groups of mounted cavalry and infantry.**

73. During the war, **the Spanish built a number of forts and settlements** to protect themselves from the many Chichimeca raids.

74. **The Chichimeca were able to successfully resist the Spanish for decades.**

75. In the 1570s, the war was not going as well for Spain as expected. **The Spanish governor-general had to write back to King Philip II for many more troops and equipment.**

76. **The Chichimeca were eventually defeated in 1590.**

77. As a result of the war, **the Spanish were able to establish a permanent foothold in central Mexico.**

78. **The Chichimeca War led to the decimation of the Chichimeca people and the destruction of their culture.**

79. **Today, very little is known about the Chichimeca people.** What we know mainly comes from the Spanish, which can be biased.

80. **The Chichimeca War is believed to have resulted in the deaths of up to eighty thousand people, mostly Chichimeca.** However, no one is certain about how many died, though most believe the total was well in excess of ten thousand.

81. **The Chichimeca War resulted in many Chichimeca people being forced to move to other regions of Mexico.**
82. **The war also led to the enslavement of thousands of Chichimeca by the Spanish.**
83. **The Aztecs regarded the Chichimeca as "uncivilized," and the name "Chichimeca" is actually an Aztec word that means "barbarian" or "uncivilized."**
84. **The Chichimeca War** had a lasting impact on the history of Mexico. It was the last great native war against the Spanish and led to a new European social, political, and economic order being imposed on the country.

85. **News traveled relatively quickly from Mexico to Spain**, considering the time and distance. Soon, many of the Spanish ruling class and a number of **important religious figures spoke out against the war** and suggested buying the Chichimeca off.

86. **The Spanish "purchased peace" with a huge sum of money**. In return, the Chichimeca promised they would not interfere with Spanish trade in their territory.
87. **The Spanish also began erecting schools and churches**. Within two generations, many of the remaining Chichimeca had become assimilated into the dominant Spanish culture.
88. **The Chichimeca War also led to the introduction of new plants and animals to new regions of Mexico**, including horses, cattle, wheat, barley, pears, apples, and figs.
89. **The Chichimeca War also led to the spread of diseases**, such as smallpox and measles, which decimated the Chichimeca population.
90. **The Chichimeca War is an important part of Mexico's history**, as it reminds us of the struggles of the indigenous people against European colonialism.

Mexican War of Independence
(1810–1821)

The Mexican War of Independence was an epic struggle between the people of Mexico and the Spanish colonial government. On September 16th, 1810, this conflict was set in motion with the cry of a **Catholic priest named Miguel Hidalgo y Costilla**. Spanning eleven years, the war was fought with a combination of conventional and guerrilla tactics and saw the introduction of various new weapons, new forms of government, and new leaders. **The Mexican War of Independence** provided the foundation for a new nation, **the United Mexican States**, and marked the beginning of a **new era for Latin America**.

91. **The Mexican War of Independence**, an epic conflict between **the people of Mexico and the Spanish colonial government,** began on September 16th, 1810.

92. **The Spanish wanted to colonize Mexico in 1519 because they believed they could find gold and silver**. They found those precious items in abundance, as well as many other resources that made Spain a wealthy nation.

93. **The struggle for independence was spearheaded by a number of Mexican revolutionaries, such as Catholic priests Miguel Hidalgo y Costilla** and **José María Morelos, Vicente Guerrero,** and **Guadalupe Victoria** (aka Manuel Félix Fernández).

94. **A number of other Latin American nations had won independence from Spain prior to the Mexican War of Independence**, including Venezuela, Paraguay, Argentina, Colombia, Peru, and Chile.

95. **The war was initiated by the cry of Miguel Hidalgo y Costilla**, a Catholic priest who made an impassioned speech at Dolores. This speech is known as **the Grito de Dolores** ("The Cry of Dolores").

96. **After Costilla's capture and execution in 1811, fellow priest José María Morelos became one of the main leaders of the revolution against the Spanish.**

97. One of the leaders of the revolution was **Josefa Ortiz de Domínguez**, also known as **La Corregidora** ("the Magistrate").

98. **Ignacio Allende**, the son of a wealthy trader, and **Mariano Matamoros**, a priest, were two others who rose to prominence during the war.

99. **Near the end of the war, former areas of Spanish Mexico became independent.** These were Guatemala, El Salvador, Honduras, Costa Rica, and Nicaragua, all of which became independent on September 15th, 1821.

100. **One of the decisive battles of the war and a Mexican victory was the Battle of Puente de Calderón** (the Battle of Calderón Bridge) in 1811.

101. **The war was fought in many parts of Mexico**, including Guanajuato, Michoacán, Oaxaca, Jalisco, and the Yucatán.

102. **The Mexican War of Independence** ended on August 24th, 1821, with the signing of **the Treaty of Córdoba**, which made Mexico an independent country.

103. **Before and after the war, Mexico was a highly stratified society.** At the top of the power pyramid were Spaniards born in Spain. Next were people of **Spanish descent born in Mexico**. The people of **"mixed" Spanish and Mexican-born Spanish heritage were the third tier**. At the bottom were the indigenous people of the country.

104. **Most of the revolutionaries were of Spanish descent who had been born in Mexico.** They were tired of being second-class citizens. **The indigenous people of Mexico remained largely without rights** or a voice in their own country.

105. **The Spanish born in Mexico were called criollos** ("creoles" in English), meaning they were of Spanish descent but born in the New World. However, the word has different meanings throughout the Western Hemisphere.

106. **The Constitution of Apatzingán was written in 1814** and was made the law of areas controlled by the revolutionaries until **it was replaced by a national constitution in 1824.**

107. **The Constitution of 1824 declared Roman Catholicism to be the state religion.** It also made guarantees about individual rights under the law. Unfortunately, there was a big difference between what was written in the constitution and reality.

108. **A new form of government gave rise to new national symbols, like the Mexican flag and the Mexican coat of arms.**

109. **The Mexican War of Independence resulted in the creation of a new nation called the United Mexican States.**

110. **Slavery was abolished in Mexico at the end of the war.**

111. The end of the war saw the emergence of political parties, namely **the Conservative Party and the Liberal Party.**

112. The war also saw the establishment of a **new capital city, Mexico City.**

113. Though it grew very slowly, **Protestantism gained new followers in Mexico** in the early 19th century. This was partly caused by exposure to Americans.

114. **This period gave birth to Mexican literature.** One of the most famous was the novel *El Periquillo Sarniento* by José Joaquín Fernández de Lizardi. The book, which is called *The Mangy Parrot* in English, is an allegory for Mexico's transition from colony to country.

115. **The United States recognized Mexican independence in 1822.**

116. **Agustín de Iturbide, who declared Mexico an independent nation in 1821, was one of the most prominent political figures of the war.** He was briefly called the emperor of Mexico before the new constitution was written.

117. **The Mexican Constitution of 1824** declared that the country would have three branches of government, and the executive branch would consist of three people elected by representatives.

118. **The war also resulted in the establishment of a new legal system** based on **the Napoleonic Code**, which was the dominant law code in Europe at the time.

119. The early 19th century saw the emergence of several new leaders in Latin America, such **as Simón Bolívar in Venezuela, José de San Martín in Argentina,** and **Bernardo O'Higgins in Chile.**

120. **The war also established a new national currency, the peso,** which is still used in Mexico today.

First Mexican Empire
(1822–1823)

From its inception in 1822, the First Mexican Empire marked a dramatic shift in the trajectory of Mexico and its people. Established as a monarchy by former royalist **general Agustín de Iturbide, the First Mexican Empire** was a brief yet influential period in Mexico's history. **Emperor Agustín I's** coronation ceremony marked the beginning of a tumultuous reign characterized by political and economic instability. Yet, despite its fragility, **the First Mexican Empire introduced reforms** that had a lasting impact on Mexico and paved the way for future generations.

121. **Agustín de Iturbide, a former general, was proclaimed emperor of Mexico** by leading military figures on May 19th, 1822.

122. **Agustín had much popular support**, although he faced opposition from representatives in Congress who wanted a republic.

123. **The First Mexican Empire only lasted a short time and was replaced by a republic in 1823.**

124. **Emperor Agustín I's lavish coronation ceremony took place in Mexico City at the Catedral Metropolitana de la Ciudad México** (the Metropolitan Cathedral of Mexico City).

125. **The fight against Spain united many Mexicans**, but after the war was over, their differences became clear.

126. **Emperor Agustín and Congress began to clash immediately because no one knew what power(s) belonged to each branch of government.**

127. **The First Mexican Empire was a monarchy**, yet the emperor held limited power. The authority of the nation was primarily held by **the Congress**, officially called **the Congress of the Union.**

128. **Congress and Emperor Agustín argued a lot**. At one point, members of Congress talked about kidnapping the emperor and his family! **Agustín responded to this threat by dismissing Congress and taking more power for himself.**

129. **In the First Mexican Empire, the Catholic Church was named the religion of the state.**

130. **Initially, the First Mexican Empire** was backed by the Catholic Church. However, that backing waned when the emperor became more authoritarian.

131. **Emperor Agustín I of Mexico implemented a policy of centralization** and vested the power of government in the emperor and his ministers.

132. **After the Mexican War of Independence, parts of the old Spanish territory of New Spain became part of Mexico**. The emperor asked these territories, which made up many of today's Central American countries, if they wanted to be part of Mexico. They refused and were let go.

133. **The First Mexican Empire passed laws restricting slavery**. The First Mexican Republic abolished it in 1829, though the practice continued in parts of the country until 1837, when it was outlawed in all regions of Mexico.

134. Mexican production, especially of its most valuable commodity, silver, dropped during **the First Mexican Empire**, leading to widespread economic hardship.

135. **Mexico had gone into considerable debt in the first years of independence** and needed to borrow more to make payments, which started a vicious cycle of borrowing, further weakening the country.

136. **The First Mexican Empire was financially fragile**, with a weak currency and hyperinflation.

137. **Agustín I was not a very good politician**, and combined with the poor state of the country, he faced growing unpopularity.

138. **Though they had mixed results, the empire period introduced economic policies focused on promoting internal trade and industrial development**. This included the encouragement of domestic production, the establishment of trade agreements with foreign countries, and the creation of a national bank to facilitate economic growth.

139. **The First Mexican Empire issued its own currency called the peso**. Some pesos were coins, while some were paper.

140. **The government began printing more and more paper money to pay its debts**, which resulted in high inflation.

141. **During the empire, opinions on education were divided**. Many wished the Catholic Church to keep its role as the main provider of education, but a growing number wished to see a secular public school system begin, which did occur after the end of the empire.

142. **The First Mexican Empire had a strong military,** including cavalry, infantry units, and a navy.

143. **The king of Spain held a lot of influence, and few nations recognized Mexico's independence. Mexico's trade suffered as a result.**

144. **Emperor Agustín I of Mexico was exiled in 1823 and replaced by a federal republic.**

145. **The First Mexican Empire** is known as a period of political and economic instability, with the peso losing its value and the government unable to pay its debts.

146. **Mexico had and still has a large indigenous population,** with many of the indigenous people living in rural areas and working as agricultural laborers.

147. **Ana María Huarte became Empress Consort** and was given the title of **Empress Ana María.** She was known for her beauty and elegance and was highly regarded in Mexican high society.

148. **After her husband's death, Ana María returned to Mexico in 1838** and dedicated herself to preserving her husband's memory.

149. **Leona Vicario** (1789–1842) was an influential journalist, activist, and poet. She supported **the Mexican independence movement** and used her writing to promote nationalist ideas. Vicario is known for her significant contributions to the Mexican press during the early 19th century.

150. **José María Heredia** (1803–1839) was a renowned **poet and writer**. He is considered one of the most important figures in Latin American Romanticism. His works often explored themes of liberty, love, and patriotism.

First Republic of Mexico
(1824–1835)

The First Republic of Mexico had a brief but transformative eleven-year history that left an indelible mark on the nation. **From recognizing the United States as a sovereign nation to abolishing slavery**, introducing the metric system, issuing paper money and coins, and establishing a bicameral legislature, this revolutionary republic sought to bring unprecedented levels of **freedom and justice to its citizens**.

151. **With its "birth" in 1824, the First Republic of Mexico broke new ground for Mexico.** Mexico became a unitary state (a united country with a powerful federal government) that sought to unite the people under **the slogan of "Union, Liberty, and Justice."**

152. **During its eleven-year history, the First Republic was led by three different** presidents who sought to bring increased levels of freedom to the people. This sometimes happened more in word than in deed.

153. **In 1835, the region of Texas declared its independence from Mexico**, sparking a struggle for power that lasted until 1836.

154. **On April 8th, 1824, this new republic enacted a new constitution that aimed to build a strong centralized government**, which was one reason the Texans later declared their independence.

155. **On December 12th, 1822, Mexico became the second nation in Latin America to recognize the United States as a sovereign nation**, the first being Colombia in June of the same year. **The United States recognized Mexico the same year**.

156. **The First Republic used the United States as a model for its structure.** Its constitution gave great autonomy to the states, much like in the US.

157. **By introducing the metric system, the First Republic of Mexico revolutionized the way people measured and understood the world.**

158. **In 1825, the First Republic of Mexico issued new paper money and coins that strengthened the nation's economy and currency.**

159. **By abolishing slavery in the early 19th century, the First Republic of Mexico** made a bold statement to the world about the importance of human rights and dignity.

160. The government of the republic included a bicameral legislature, **the Chamber of Deputies, and the Senate.**

161. In an effort to bring the nation together, **a national postal system was established** in 1830.

162. To ensure fairness and accuracy, **Mexico adopted a new system of weights and measures** in 1831.

163. **During the First Republic, the groundwork of the Mexican public education system was laid**, which was followed by the passage of significant laws by other Mexican regimes from 1856 to 1867.

164. **On March 28th, 1833, the First Republic of Mexico issued a decree that abolished the use of indigenous languages** in government, education, and church and imposed Spanish as the national language.

165. **The First Republic of Mexico constructed a series of roads** to tie the country together.

166. Railroads became an important way to move goods and people. **Mexico constructed railways throughout the country,** though many of them were controlled by rich criollo families or American and British investors.

167. **The University of Mexico is the oldest university in North America**. During the First Republic, it opened its doors to more people, but it was not open to all Mexicans, especially the poor.

168. To ensure financial stability, **the First Republic of Mexico introduced a new federal tax system.** Most people ignored its regulations, and the government was too new and weak to enforce the law.

169. **In 1832, in an effort to protect writers and inventors, the First Republic of Mexico enacted a national system of copyright law.**

170. **Mexico had public hospitals since Spanish times**, both for Europeans and for indigenous people. Under the republic, the number of hospitals in Mexico increased.

171. **In 1833, the Federal Labor Law was passed**, introducing protections for workers for the first time. Compared to labor laws today, the 1833 law was simple and did not offer the same kind of protections, but it was an important beginning.

172. **The Mexican state included the territory we know as Mexico today but also Texas, Arizona, New Mexico, and a large part of California**. All of these territories were difficult to govern from Mexico City, which is one reason the Mexican government's hold on them became so weak.

173. **The Banco de Avío, an early centralized national bank**, was established in 1830.

174. The Mexican War of Independence **hero Guadalupe Victoria** was **the first president of Mexico** (1824–1829)

175. **Guadalupe Victoria was the only president of the republic who was not overthrown and replaced,** something that usually happened by the military.

176. **There were nine presidents of the First Republic**, but those nine "vacancies" were filled by only six people, as **Valentín Gómez Farías and General de Santa Anna** replaced each other frequently between 1833 and 1835.

177. Though **Antonio López de Santa Anna** was in and out of office, he dominated Mexican politics from 1833 until 1846, sometimes while he was in office and sometimes as a military dictator in all but name.

178. **The Mexican Constitution of 1824 gave the right to vote to any man over the age of eighteen,** provided they were in good standing, which meant known criminals and anyone else the people in power wished to limit.

179. **In parts of Mexico, far from the capital, indigenous people revolted against the government because of the discrimination and prejudice of authorities**. One of the biggest uprisings happened in California in 1824 when **the Chumash tribe** rose up against the government.

180. Though some important changes were made during this period, **the First Republic of Mexico was characterized by political instability and frequent changes in government**. It experienced several presidents and numerous uprisings and conflicts during its existence.

Texas War of Independence
(1835–1836)

From the Battle of Gonzales to the decisive victory at the Battle of San Jacinto, the Texas War of Independence was a complex and tumultuous struggle. The Texans, made up mostly of volunteers who were ill-prepared for battle, faced off against the large **Mexican Army led by Santa Anna**. Heroes were made, battles were fought, and a nation was born. This chapter will explore the events that led to **the Texas War of Independence**, the battles and other events of the war, and the lasting legacy of this critical piece **of Mexican and American history**.

181. **The Texas War of Independence began on October 2nd, 1835, with the Battle of Gonzales.**

182. **The Texas War of Independence** was fought between Mexican forces led by **General Antonio López de Santa Anna** and Texan forces led by **General Sam Houston**.

183. **Sam Houston was governor of Tennessee from 1827 to 1829 and eventually became the first president of Texas in 1836.** He would serve another term from 1841 to 1844.

184. **Many Americans headed to Texas for cheap land during the Republic of Mexico.** At first, the Mexicans welcomed this, as it brought some wealth and stability. But when more Americans came and set up their own way of running things, Mexico decided to stop selling them land, setting the stage for **the Texas War of Independence**.

185. **The Texas War of Independence was a result of the increasing tensions between Mexico and the settlers of Texas over land rights and slavery.** Most Texans were pro-slavery, whereas the Mexican government had abolished slavery years before.

186. **The Texan army was mostly made up of volunteers from the United States**, including many former American soldiers. They were poorly equipped and ill-prepared for battle when it began.

187. Many people with Mexican or **indigenous Mexican heritage decided they preferred being part of Texas instead of Mexico,** which had become a dictatorship under Santa Anna.

History of Mexico

188. **Stephen F. Austin was known as the "Father of Texas"** and was an important leader in the Texas War of Independence.

189. **Many people believe the Texas state flag was designed by Dr. Charles B. Stewart, an important politician**, but others believe it **was designed by Peter Krag**, an artist from Austin. The flag was adopted as the national flag of Texas on January 25th, 1839.

190. **James Fannin was an American officer** who moved to Texas from Georgia in 1834. He was an early leader in the Texas War of Independence but **was executed by Mexican forces in the Goliad massacre**.

191. **The Goliad massacre was an event during the Texas War of Independence** in which over four hundred Texan prisoners of war were executed by **Colonel José Nicolás de la Portilla** because of an order issued **by Santa Anna** in which all foreigners (meaning Americans) were to be treated as bandits and executed.

192. The cannonball from the **"Come and Take It"** cannon was the first shot fired in **the Battle of Gonzales,** which began the Texas War of Independence. The local Mexican detachment demanded the Texans surrender the cannon, as it could be used against the Mexicans. The Texans refused.

193. **Davy Crockett was an adventurer and former US Congressman** from Tennessee who died defending the Alamo.

194. **The Battle of the Alamo was a thirteen-day siege**, lasting from February 23rd, 1836, to March 6th, 1836, which resulted in a Texan defeat. This is where we get the saying, "Remember the Alamo!"

195. **William B. Travis was the commander of the Texan forces** at the Battle of the Alamo and died while defending the fort.

196. **The Battle of the Alamo** is remembered as one of the most heroic stands in history, with the Texan defenders fighting against overwhelming odds.

197. **The Texan forces at the Battle of the Alamo were greatly outnumbered**, with only about two hundred men facing off against Santa Anna's army. Historians estimate that Santa Anna's force ranged between 1,500 and 6,000 men, though the lower figure is probably more accurate.

198. A famed American frontiersman, slave trader, and adventurer named **James Bowie took part in the war.** He was famous for carrying an over-sized knife, which became known as **the Bowie knife** after his death at **the Battle of the Alamo**.

199. **The victory at the Battle of Concepción** (October 28th, 1835) was the first victory for Texan forces. The Texans were led by **James Fannin and James ("Jim") Bowie**.

200. **Juan Seguin was an important Tejano leader** in the Texas War of Independence who fought for Texan independence. Tejanos are Spanish-speaking Texans.

201. **The Texian Navy was created by the Texan government** and played a small but important role in the Texas War of Independence. The navy held its own against the more modern Mexican Navy at the Battle of Campeche off the coast of the Yucatán Peninsula.

202. **The Battle of Coleto** in March 1836 was a decisive victory for Texan forces and led to the capture of Goliad, a town that had been fought over since the beginning of the war.

203. **The Texas Rangers were a paramilitary force established** in November 1835 to protect American settlers from Native American attacks. They played a significant role in key battles like the Battle of San Jacinto.

204. **The Battle of San Jacinto** was fought on April 21st, 1836, and was the final battle of **the Texas War of Independence**.

205. **The Battle of San Jacinto**, which was the pivotal battle of the Texas War of Independence, lasted eighteen minutes!

206. **Santa Anna was captured by Texan forces at the Battle of San Jacinto.**

207. Santa Anna was known as the **"Napoleon of the West"** and was the president of Mexico, although he gave up the position to lead the Mexican forces in the war.

208. **The Treaty of Velasco officially ended the Texas War of Independence** and recognized the independence of the Republic of Texas.

209. **The Texas Constitution was adopted in March 1836** and established the Republic of Texas as an independent nation.

210. **The Republic of Texas was an independent nation for nine years before being voluntarily annexed by the United States in 1845.**

The Centralist Mexican Republic
(1835–1846)

In 1836, the Centralist Mexican Republic was established, marking ten years of turbulent and transformative change. The nation saw the abolition of slavery, a new constitution, **the rise of President Antonio López de Santa Anna**, and an array of reforms that shaped Mexico's history, culture, and economy. **The Centralist Mexican Republic** was the precursor of much progress in the Western Hemisphere, foretelling many changes that would affect neighboring countries. Here are some key facts about this formidable era in **Mexico's history.**

211. **In 1835, the First Mexican Republic ended**. Bad tax collection policies, inflation, constant power struggles, and the troubles in Texas and elsewhere led to the government's collapse.

212. **The Constitution of 1824 was nullified, and a new constitution called the Seven Laws** was put in its place.

213. One man dominated this period: General (and sometimes President) **Antonio López de Santa Anna.** Many historians have likened him to a king or dictator.

214. **For ten years, the nation was divided into nineteen states and four territories**, with the military holding most of the power in the country.

215. **The Mexican-American War** wrought havoc on the political, military, and especially the economic life of Mexico, causing widespread hardship.

216. **Changes were introduced**, such as the abolition of communal landholding, **a new and centralized currency called the "real,"** and a new system of education.

217. **The president was given the authority to appoint and dismiss state governors**. He also often employed the military to silence opposition.

218. **The Seven Laws** (*Siete Leyes*) tried to create a strong national government as opposed to the Constitution of 1824, which gave more power to local and state governments.

219. **The weakness of the First Republic's government and the defeat in the war with the US led to the end of the First Republic.**

220. **Mexico was the first Latin American nation to form diplomatic relations with the United States**.

221. **European Enlightenment ideas and the Roman Catholic Church had a considerable effect on the nation's politics and laws**. Generally speaking, these two ways of thinking and looking at the world were opposed to each other.

222. **In Mexico, a split began between liberals**, who looked on Europe and the US as a model, and conservatives, who took their cue from **the Catholic Church** and monarchies in Europe.

223. **The Conservative Party dominated** the years of **the Centralist Mexican Republic**.

224. **Santa Anna gained power after commanding a unit in the Mexican War of Independence**. Military officers were not allowed to hold the presidential office, so Santa Anna "resigned" repeatedly.

225. **Santa Anna was in and out of power for years**. In 1855, he was forced into exile, which lasted until 1874. **He lived in Cuba** and, surprisingly, in the US, his former enemy, as well as Colombia and the Virgin Islands.

226. **Santa Anna tried to re-enter politics unsuccessfully** and was an unsuccessful businessman. He was buried with full military honors when he died in his homeland in 1876.

227. **Under Santa Anna, the Catholic Church was allowed to retain its privileges** and vast tracts of land in return for a monthly "donation" to the state. Some of this money made it into the hands of Santa Anna.

228. **Despite the power and influence of the Catholic Church**, Mexicans enjoyed freedom of worship during this period.

229. **The rebellion in Texas and Santa Anna's harsh treatment of captured Texans caused other parts of Mexico to rise in rebellion against centralized authority**.

230. **A rebellion in the military** against the new centralized structure of the government took place in 1838, which was defeated the next year.

231. The leader of the 1838 revolt, **General José de Urrea**, broke out of prison to join another revolt against the government, which saw fighting in the streets of Mexico City. **Santa Anna**, who had already been in and out of power twice, came back and **formed a military dictatorship in 1842.**

232. **Santa Anna ordered another constitution to be drawn up, the Bases Orgánicas, or "Organic Basis"** (of the nation), in 1843. This constitution gave even more power to the president.

233. **The Bases Orgánicas also provided for an expanded public school system, something that was important to Santa Anna.**

234. **The Centralist Mexican Republic** faced significant opposition from federalist forces and regional governments, particularly in states like **Texas, Yucatán, and Zacatecas**. These regions sought to maintain their autonomy and resisted the centralization efforts.

235. **In 1842, Santa Anna attempted to reform and recentralize the collection of federal taxes,** something that led to widespread anger and his temporary downfall.

236. **Spain finally recognized the independence of Mexico in 1836.**

237. **The Centralist Mexican Republic** formed the first true standing army of Mexico. Previously, it had relied on local militias.

238. From 1838 to 1839, **the Pastry War with France was fought over trade issues** and corruption in the Mexican government.

239. **France seized the city of Veracruz and blockaded Mexican ports until the British brokered a peace agreement between the two countries.**

240. Foreign intervention, government infighting, civil unrest, and resistance to federal rule by states and indigenous people all contributed to **the downfall of the Centralist Mexican Republic.**

Caste War of Yucatán
(1847–1901)

Let's look at some interesting facts surrounding **the Caste War of Yucatán. This war lasted over fifty years and saw the Maya and the Mexican government fight each other.** The Mexican government's endeavor to quell the uprising resulted in the deaths of thousands of Maya and the displacement of thousands more. **The Caste War left a lasting impact on the Yucatán region.** Let's discover why.

241. **The Caste War of Yucatán began on July 30th, 1847.**

242. The Caste War was **a conflict between the Maya people of the Yucatán Peninsula and the Mexican government.**

243. There were actually two revolts in **the Yucatán Peninsula** that began in the 1840s. One was **led by criollo leaders** who wanted to establish an independent state. **The other was led by the Maya,** who wanted their own independent nation, free from the Mexican government and the criollos' discrimination.

244. **The Maya army initially fought with machetes, spears, and bows and arrows since the region was poor and lacked access to modern weapons.**

245. In an effort to outwit their adversaries, **the Maya forces utilized guerrilla tactics** like ambushes in the deep forests.

246. In 1846, **some Maya rose up against the Mexican authorities.** When one of its leaders, Manuel Antonio Ay, was executed by the government, most of **the Maya people in the Yucatán rose up in revolt, starting the Caste War.**

247. **Cecilio Chí and Jacinto Pat were among the most influential leaders of the Maya forces.**

248. In the midst of the Caste War, **Maya forces proclaimed an independent nation, the Republic of Chan Santa Cruz.**

249. **The Republic of Chan Santa Cruz had a government and constitution of its own.**

250. The war was not continuous. For a time in the late 19th century, **various Mexican governments recognized that Maya Yucatán had its own government,** but changes in leadership and policy changed this in the early 20th century when a renewed government effort succeeded in absorbing **Chan Santa Cruz** back into Mexico.

251. **The Caste War** caused recurring destruction, economic hardship, and the displacement of many Maya.

252. **The Mexican government's endeavor to suppress the Maya uprising resulted in the deaths of thousands of Maya.**

253. **In 1901, Mexican forces took over the Maya people's proclaimed capital of Chan Santa Cruz and the surrounding area.** Most people knew the war was over, but it did not officially end until 1915, when the leadership of the Maya relented.

254. **After the war was over, some Maya demands were met**, like more autonomy for the region than it had before the revolt began.

255. **The Caste War was a major influence in the diminishment of the Maya population in the Yucatán region.**

256. **The Caste War** caused a loss of economic and political power for the Maya people.

257. **The Caste War caused the loss of many traditional Maya customs and beliefs.**

258. Before the war, **the Mexican government sought to incorporate the Maya people into mainstream Mexican culture using intimidation and force.** That gradually changed in the early 20th century when peaceful dialogue between the two sides developed.

259. **The Caste War is seen by many as a symbol of indigenous resistance** to oppression and exploitation and a testament to their endurance.

260. **The three most famous Maya leaders of the time—Manuel Ay, Cecilio Chí, and Jacinto Pat—all** died before the war was over. Ay was executed by the Mexican government, which was the spark that set off the war, and both **Chi and Pat were assassinated by rivals.** Still, all three are regarded as the leaders and spirit behind the Maya independence movement.

Mexican-American War
(1846–1848)

The Mexican-American War changed the course of history. In this chapter, you'll learn many new things about this conflict, including the role camels played and the **Americans who fought in Mexico who would later be leaders in the US Civil War**. The war resulted in a significant shift in the balance of power in the Southwest, with **the US gaining control of much of the region**. Let's dive in!

261. **The Mexican-American War** began in 1846 and ended two years later with **the Treaty of Guadalupe Hidalgo**.

262. **The United States and Mexico became embroiled in a conflict** due to disputes over their shared border and possession of Texas, which had become part of the US in 1845.

263. Despite having an advantage in numbers, **the Mexican Army was hampered by a lack of modern equipment and weaponry.**

264. **The US Army was led by General Zachary Taylor and General Winfield Scott**.

265. **The Mexican Army was commanded by Antonio López de Santa Anna** and was composed of professional soldiers, militia, and civilian volunteers.

266. **Santa Anna had been forced into exile in 1845 but wanted to return to his home country.** He promised the Americans that if they let him pass through their blockade, he would lead Mexico out of the war.

267. **When Santa Anna arrived in Mexico, he changed his mind, causing US forces to invade Mexico City to defeat Santa Anna and the Mexicans.**

268. The war was fought in a number of locations, including the present-day states of **California, New Mexico, Arizona, Texas, and parts of Colorado**, as well as in the deserts, mountains, and **plains of Mexico**.

269. **The Mexican Army suffered from a lack of supplies**, including food and ammunition.

History of Mexico

270. **In Mexico, the US Army was known for its brutal tactics**, such as burning villages and crops.
271. **The US forces were aided by Seminole, Creek, and Cherokee scouts.**
272. **The US Army made use of camels for the first time** in survey and reconnaissance missions.
273. **The training base used by the "Camel Corps" was in Camp Verde, Texas.**
274. **The US Navy was able to transport troops and supplies** and shell Mexican positions and cities on the coasts.

275. **The Mexican forces used guerrilla tactics.** They employed hit-and-run tactics, such as ambushes and raids.
276. **The US Army's tactics were only a little different**, relying on a combination of siege warfare and maneuvers to outwit its opponents.

277. **The war caused the displacement of many Native American tribes from their ancestral lands,** resulting in a major shift in the balance of power in the Southwest, with the US gaining control of much of the region.

278. **At first, many Spanish-speaking people in California supported the Americans**, but the atrocities and outrageous behavior of many American volunteer units caused them to rebel. They were defeated in **the Battle of Providencia** near modern-day Los Angeles.

279. **The US Navy blockaded Mexican ports** and prohibited Mexican shipping during the war, disrupting Mexico's economy.

280. **The Mexican cavalry was made up of skilled lancers**. (A lance was a spear designed to be used by a mounted warrior or cavalry soldier. It was used in medieval times as well.)

281. **The US cavalry was made up of dragoons armed with sabers and pistols.**

282. Many American soldiers who later became famous in the US Civil War saw action in **the Mexican-American War**. These included **Ulysses S. Grant, Robert E. Lee, and Thomas J. "Stonewall" Jackson.**

283. The president of the United States during the war was **James K. Polk**, who had promised he would only serve one term if his major goals were met. One of these goals was the conquest of Mexican territory in the west.

284. **The US Army was also aided by a large number of volunteers**, many of whom had fought in the Texas War of Independence.

285. The Tennessee Volunteers made history. **The University of Tennessee still calls its sports teams the "Vols."**

286. **Not all Americans were for the war.** Some believed it to be purely a war of conquest. One of these people was Congressman and future **President Abraham Lincoln.**

287. **The war resulted in the death of an estimated six thousand to twenty-five thousand Mexicans, including civilians.**

288. **American deaths totaled 1,733 men killed in action.** However, over eleven thousand died from disease.

289. **Many native people who had lived in California under Mexican rule were pushed out of the territory or killed when the United States took over.**

290. Estimates of **indigenous Californians killed** by white settlers and militiamen in California run between nine thousand and sixteen thousand.

291. **The Mexican-American War was the first in which the US Army used the new Colt revolver.**

292. **Winfield Scott, the overall US commander**, surrounded the Mexican coast with US ships, preventing overseas supplies from reaching Mexico.

293. **At the beginning of the US Civil War, Scott came up with the North's Anaconda Plan,** which did much the same thing to the Confederacy.

294. **The US Navy did not see any real ship-to-ship combat in the war.** Mexico's navy only existed on paper.

295. **The American victory resulted in the acquisition of over 500,000 square miles of land,** including Texas, California, Arizona, and New Mexico.

296. **After the war was won, the new treaty granted US citizens the right to acquire land in Mexico and Mexicans in the US the right to become citizens.**

297. Despite being a hero in the Mexican-American War and playing a vital role **in the Battle of Chapultepec, Ulysses Grant** later condemned the Mexican-American War and said, "To this day, (I) regard the war which resulted as one of the most unjust ever waged by a stronger against a weaker nation."

298. **US Commodore John Sloat**, who has streets, parks, and other places named for him in California, seized San Francisco from Mexico on July 9th, 1846. Other places throughout Northern California were taken over by American settlers at about the same time.

299. **The Maya in the Yucatán had closer relations with the US than they did with the Mexican government.** The US Navy used the Yucatán coast to land supplies.

300. **In the First Battle of Tabasco**, along the Mexican coast, **American naval officer Matthew C. Perry,** who would later become famous as the man that opened Japan to the outside world, was defeated when he attempted to land sailors to seize a number of towns along the coast.

The Reform War
(1858–1861)

The Reform War of the mid-19th century was a monumental turning point in **Mexican history,** ushering in a wave of social, political, and economic reforms that had far-reaching consequences. **From the introduction of a new currency to the emergence of a new type of nationalism, the Reform War gave birth to a new Mexican identity.** Let's look at some of the facts about this era!

301. **The Reform War was actually a civil war.** It was a major turning point in Mexican history, leading to the downfall of the conservative forces and the rise of the liberal forces.

302. **The war was triggered by the enactment of the Mexican Constitution of 1857**, which aimed to establish a more secular and centralized government and curtail the power of **the Catholic Church**.

303. **The liberal faction of the government, led by President Benito Juárez**, supported the new constitution and sought to implement its reforms, including **the nationalization of church properties and the separation of church and state.**

304. **The conservatives opposed the 1857 Constitution**. They were backed **by the Catholic Church and led by General Miguel Miramón.** They sought to preserve the traditional privileges and influence of the church.

305. **As a result of the Reform War, many Mexicans saw their fortunes destroyed**, leading to poverty for many.

306. **Because of corruption and mismanagement, the Mexican government found itself so strapped for cash during the Reform War** that it was forced to print paper money, which eventually became worthless.

307. **Liberals in the country wished to see the power of the military**, the Catholic Church, large landowners, and foreigners reduced in Mexico.

308. **At the start of the war, the Liberal Party and its support was located in the center of the country, including Mexico City.** Conservative support was strongest in the countryside and the north and south.

309. **The United States supported the Liberal Party** and its policies during the Reform War, while France, Spain, and Britain supported the Conservative Party.

310. **There were many issues separating Mexicans from one another.** All of their problems came to light during the fight over the contents of the 1857 Constitution. The main issue was how strong the central government was going to be in respect to the states.

311. Just before the Reform War, in 1854, a new national anthem emerged, **the Himno Nacional Mexicano,** which is the national anthem of the country today.

312. In the mid-19th century, Mexican writers began to make a name for themselves in the Spanish-speaking world, such as **Vicente Riva Palacio, Ignacio Galván**, and many others.

313. **The Reform War also saw the emergence of a new type of nationalism in Mexico**, one that was based on liberalism and "people power."

314. **The Reform War led to the reform of the Mexican Supreme Court,** which was tasked with the oversight of the judiciary system. The Supreme Court had previously been firmly under the president's control.

315. The famous (and sometimes infamous) **Federales, a police-type force** of the Mexican Army tasked with maintaining public order and protecting citizens, was established at this time.

Though the Federales are now a unique unit of the Mexican police and founded in 1999, the term Federales was initially used by Americans to describe the original force and those that came after it.

316. **Many bloody battles took place during the Reform War**. Initially, the conservatives had the edge, but by the end of the war, conservative infighting, foreign aid, and the desire for change among many Mexicans gave the edge to the liberals, who won the conflict and set up a new government in 1860.

317. **The war lasted for four years, from 1857 to 1861**, and resulted in considerable devastation and loss of life. It caused political instability and economic hardship in Mexico, exacerbating existing social divisions.

318. **The damage done to the country's infrastructure during the war led to an economic downturn**, which gradually strengthened the conservatives, who sought support from the conservative emperor of France, Napoleon III.

319. **The Reform War witnessed significant foreign intervention. France, under Napoleon III,** took advantage of the internal conflict to invade Mexico in 1861 and establish the short-lived French-imposed regime known as the **Second Mexican Empire**.

320. The Reform War also saw the emergence of the peso again, which was designed to promote economic stability and growth. **The peso replaced the real.**

321. **Additionally, the Reform War led to the establishment of a new system of land reform,** which sought to redistribute land more equitably. Much land was taken from the Catholic Church, which had controlled not just the land but also employment on it.

322. **This conflict also saw the introduction of a new system of education,** which was designed to create a more literate population, one separate from the ideas of Catholicism. The church had dominated what education there was in Mexico until this time.

323. **The Reform War saw the emergence of a more organized and professional army in Mexico,** one that was better trained and better equipped than its predecessors.

324. **The Reform War resulted in the adoption of a new legal system** in Mexico known as the *Ley Lerdo* ("Lerdo Law"), which sought to limit the power of the Catholic Church, among other things.

325. **Benito Juárez was elected president of Mexico in 1861.** Juárez was a populist who had great appeal among the common people and loudly supported national pride, not just pride in the upper ruling classes.

326. **Juárez was the first indigenous president of Mexico and the first native person to hold power in the post-colonial era.** Most Mexicans consider **Benito Juárez** a hero today, though not all of his reforms were successful.

327. **This conflict brought about a new system of government**, which sought to limit the power of the executive and give more power to the people.

328. **At the end of the Reform War, a new type of foreign policy emerged in Mexico** that sought to distance Mexico from the European powers and instead focus on the Americas.

329. **The Reform War also led to the abolition of debt peonage,** which had been a major problem in Mexico prior to the war. Debt peonage means that people worked off debts with labor.

330. **Additionally, the Reform War saw the emergence of a new type of economy in Mexico.** This new economy was based on free trade and economic liberalization, much like more prominent Western capitalist societies of the time.

The Second Mexican Empire
(1864–1867)

Another empire? Yes! The Second Mexican Empire was an attempt to restore order to a chaotic nation. Established in 1864, **this short-lived monarchy was funded by the French government** and heavily supported by the conservative segment of the Mexican population. **Emperor Maximilian I**, the sole monarch of **the Second Mexican Empire,** initiated a series of reforms. However, his reign came to an abrupt end. Discover how, as well as **the empire's impact on Mexico.**

331. **The Second Mexican Empire** was established in 1864 and ended in 1867. Thus, it was a short period of monarchical rule.

332. **Chaos and civil war were the impetus for the Second Mexican Empire**, which was created in an attempt to restore order.

333. **Benito Juárez was forced out of the capital, but he never left the country.**

334. **Maximilian I was the only monarch of the Second Mexican Empire.**

335. **Emperor Maximilian I's reign over the Second Mexican Empire was heavily supported by the conservative elite,** who had struggled in the Reform War.

336. **The conservative Catholic Church also supported the Second Mexican Empire.**

337. As expected, **the Second Mexican Empire** was vigorously opposed by the liberal forces in Mexico.

338. **Emperor Napoleon III of France**, nephew of Napoleon Bonaparte, wanted to grow France's influence overseas. **He largely funded the effort to bring Maximilian to power.**

339. Maximilian was a member of the Habsburg family, whose members sat on the thrones of Spain and Austria.

340. **During the Second Mexican Empire, the US was involved in fighting its own civil war and was not able to prevent France's interference in Mexico.** The US continued to support the republican government, though.

341. **Empress Carlota, Maximilian's wife, was a key figure in the Second Mexican Empire.** When Maximilian was gone from the capital, he made his wife regent until he returned.

342. **Political unrest and turmoil were hallmarks of the short-lived monarchy.**
343. **A railroad from Mexico City to the important city of Veracruz was created** during the Second Mexican Empire.
344. In 1866, facing a possible war in Europe and not willing to fight the now re-united United States, **Napoleon III withdrew French troops, including the famous French Foreign Legion, and financial support from Maximilian.**

345. **Treason charges stemming from the emperor's support from France resulted in his execution,** bringing the Second Mexican Empire to a close.
346. **Empress Carlota was in Europe attempting to get more aid for the empire when her husband was killed by a firing squad.**

347. **Carlota spent the rest of her life in seclusion in Europe.** She died in 1927.
348. **The execution of Maximilian caused outrage in Europe,** leading to strained diplomatic relations between Mexico and several European countries.
349. **The Second Mexican Empire's collapse was a significant blow to European ambitions of expanding their influence in the Americas.**
350. After deposing Maximilian I, liberal forces, which favored a republic, **ended the Second Mexican Empire in 1867.**
351. **The Mexican Congress officially dissolved the Second Mexican Empire in 1867.**
352. **Mexico faced significant challenges in rebuilding and recovering from the war** and the period of foreign intervention.
353. **Maximilian and Carlota's story has inspired literature, art, and films,** contributing to their enduring place in popular culture.
354. **The events of the Second Mexican Empire had a lasting impact on Mexican nationalism and the country's sense of identity**. After this period, Mexican nationalism increased dramatically throughout the country.
355. **Despite its foreign origins, music brought by the French influenced Mexican culture to this day.** Some say mariachi music has its roots in what the French called "marriage music," when Mexican musicians were hired to play both Mexican music and European waltzes.

Expansion of Industrialization
(1890-1940)

The period of industrialization between 1890 and 1940 saw Mexico undergo a drastic transformation in its infrastructure, industries, and technology. Let's look at some key facts about this important era in **Mexico's history**, as well as explore the causes and implications of Mexico's industrial revolution.

356. **Mexico experienced significant industrialization in the period from 1890 to 1940.**

357. **In 1895, a modern railroad was built from Mexico City to Puebla.**

358. **Mexico began to focus on industrialization** to increase economic growth. It had watched the US and Europe grow their economies through industrial development.

359. **The government increased investment in infrastructure,** building improved roads and railways.

360. **Mexico passed a series of internal and external tariffs** (taxes on goods) that were partly successful.

361. **Smaller Mexican businesses were hurt by internal tariffs,** but some larger businesses, like the textile industry, benefited because foreign textile goods were taxed at a high rate.

362. **The government provided subsidies to encourage the growth of Mexican industry.**

363. **Mexican industrial growth** was hindered by a significant amount of corruption in government and business.

364. **Mexico began to produce consumer goods for other countries,** such as clothing and furniture, but most Mexicans had a hard time affording more than the necessities. This situation began to change in Mexico's biggest cities by the start of the 20th century.

365. **The number of factories in Mexico increased** significantly during the period of industrialization.

366. **Mexico's manufacturing sector was dominated by textiles, food products, and mining.**

367. During this period, **Mexico became a major producer** of petroleum and other minerals.
368. **Mexico opened its doors to foreign investment**, especially from 1876 to 1911, leading to increased economic growth.
369. **The government established a national bank in 1925** to help direct and coordinate the economy.
370. In the early 20th century, **Mexico began its own steel, cement, and other industries for construction,** which aided in the country's economic growth and lessened its dependence on other countries.
371. **Automobile production began in Mexico in 1925.**
372. **Ford opened a plant in the San Lazaro** neighborhood of Mexico City in 1925.

373. **Mexico also began to produce many kinds of chemicals and paper.**
374. The government encouraged **the development of new industries**, such as the production of electricity. It invested heavily in power plants and electrical infrastructure.
375. **The government also invested in irrigation projects to improve agricultural production,** which helped the country become a major exporter of fruits and vegetables to the US.

376. **The number of workers in the industrial sector increased** from 600,000 in 1890 to 1.2 million in 1930.
377. **The number of factories in Mexico increased** from 1,600 in 1900 to 4,000 in 1930.
378. **Mexico's industrial production increased** from 4.2 billion pesos in 1900 to 12.5 billion pesos in 1929.
379. **The number of workers in the mining sector increased** from 30,000 in 1900 to 100,000 in 1930.
380. **The number of workers in the oil industry increased** from four thousand in 1900 to seventeen thousand in 1930.
381. **The number of workers in the textile industry increased** from twenty thousand in 1900 to seventy-two thousand in 1930.
382. **Mexico's industrial output increased** by an average of 5.5 percent each year between 1890 and 1930.

383. **Mexico had the fourth-largest economy in Latin America** in 1930.

384. In 1938, **President Lazaro Cárdenas nationalized the Mexican oil industry**, which meant the government took over all oil production and sales in the country. This move also expelled the US companies that had become very influential in Mexico.

385. **The number of factories in Mexico increased** from 1,600 in 1900 to 4,000 in 1930.

386. **Copper mining grew** in importance as the number of electrical products and the use of electricity increased. Copper is an excellent conductor of electricity.

387. Despite many improvements and the growth in wealth, **most Mexicans did not see great improvements in their living and working conditions**, which led to widespread unrest in the late 19th century and early 20th century.

388. **Mexico also established a national aviation industry** in the 1920s, which helped to further facilitate trade and transportation.

389. During the industrial revolution of the 1930s, **Mexico was one of the first countries in Latin America to develop its own steel industry.**

390. **Mexico's industrialization was heavily concentrated in the northern part of the country,** particularly in the states of Chihuahua, Coahuila, and Nuevo León.

391. **Mexico's main exports were minerals and petroleum**, although the manufacturing sector also experienced significant growth.

392. **Mexico's industrialization was heavily reliant on the importation of foreign technology and capital goods,** especially from the United States.

393. **The Rockefeller family from the US was heavily invested in Mexico's industrialization** during this period.

394. **US financial involvement in Mexico** caused great resentment among the poor and Mexican nationalists, causing tension between the two countries.

395. **The period of industrialization saw the emergence of a powerful elite class** comprised of large landowners, industrialists, and financiers who controlled much of the country's wealth and resources.

History of Mexico

The Mexican Revolution
(1910–1920)

The Mexican Revolution of 1910 erupted in a blaze of fury as insurgents led by **Francisco Ignacio Madero and Emiliano Zapata** challenged the rule of **Porfirio Díaz**. As the tumult spread across the country, legendary figures were born, inspiring thousands. **The heroes of the revolution are still remembered and revered today**, and their legacies remain alive in the Mexican people's hearts.

396. **In 1910, a group of insurgents led by Francisco Ignacio Madero initiated hostilities against the Díaz administration**, launching what would become known as **the Mexican Revolution**.

397. **Francisco Ignacio Madero had run for president against Díaz** and had been jailed for a time.

398. **Díaz had been in power since the late 1870s** and had opened the country up to large foreign companies.

399. **Corruption, abuse of workers and farmers, and Díaz's refusal to abide by democratic principles led to war.**

400. The revolutionary forces were able to defeat the forces of Porfirio Díaz after a series of battles, culminating in **the Battle of Ciudad Juárez** in 1911.

401. A major player in the upheaval was **Emiliano Zapata**. He was an instrumental figure in the formation of **the Liberation Army of the South** in 1911.

402. **Pancho Villa** was another famous revolutionary. For a time, from 1914 to 1915, the US considered him **the leader of Mexico**.

403. **The US exercised significant influence during this period and launched raids into Mexico to try and catch Pancho Villa**, who had turned against the new government and launched raids into the US, partially in response to US support of **Victoriano Huerta** and interference in Mexican affairs.

404. **Huerta initially fought for Madero**, but he turned on the president during the Ten Tragic Days, the name given to Huerta's coup.

405. Two future American military heroes, **John J. Pershing**, who led the US Army in WWI, and **George Patton**, who led an army in WWII, **took part in the fight against Villa** and his men.

406. **Venustiano Carranza** had been an ally of **Porfirio Díaz** but turned against him and became an important leader of the revolution. When he became president in 1917, many believed he did not enact the reforms the revolutionaries had fought for.

407. **The Constitution of 1917 guaranteed religious freedom and gender equality for Mexicans.**

408. Women, such as **Juana Belén Gutiérrez de Mendoza and Petra Herrera**, played a notable role in the revolution, fighting side by side with their male counterparts.

409. **Peasant rebellions against wealthy landowners increased during the revolution**, though they were frequently met with harsh repression.

410. **The overthrow of Díaz created a power vacuum** that many Mexican revolutionaries attempted to fill.

411. **Madero's government was overthrown by General Huerta**, who had the support of the United States and many Mexican generals.

412. **Huerta also had the support of the German Empire**, which was just beginning to find its feet on the world stage.

413. **Huerta's coup only made the war worse**, and Huerta was forced to resign after just a year and a half in power.

414. **Huerta would flee the country**. He lived in Spain for a time but eventually moved to the US. There, he conspired with the Germans during World War I, which led to his arrest. He died in jail.

415. In the north, near the US border, **Villa's forces were able to overcome conservative forces in Ciudad Juárez.**

416. **The Battle of Zacatecas in 1914** was a crucial success for the revolutionaries, allowing them to take control of Mexico City.

417. **Newspapers increased during the Mexican Revolution**, allowing revolutionary leaders to communicate their ideas.

418. Numerous revolutionary leaders, including **Francisco Madero and Emiliano Zapata**, were assassinated during the struggle.

419. **Emiliano Zapata, a popular revolutionary, was assassinated in 1919** when he was ambushed by Mexican Army forces.

420. **The United States offered military support** to the revolutionaries, providing them with arms and ammunition.

421. After many years of fighting, assassinations, and destruction, **many of the factions fighting in the war began to negotiate an end to the fighting.**

422. The revolution culminated in the election of **Álvaro Obregón as president** in 1920.

423. The Obregón government sought to preserve the accomplishments of the revolution, including the land reforms enshrined in **the Constitution of 1917**.

424. **Obregón's government brought stability to the country** and helped to catalyze Mexico's modernization.

425. **The revolution also saw the proliferation of labor unions** that strived to improve working conditions and wages for workers.

426. **The revolution inspired a new generation of Mexican artists**, writers, and intellectuals, such as Diego Rivera (1886–1957). These thinkers sought to create a new Mexican identity.

427. **"Mexican muralism" became popular at this time,** and it still is today. Many muralists, both then and now, concern themselves with social justice issues.

428. **The corrido** (a ballad) was **a popular form of music**. It praised the heroes of the revolution, and its songs helped spread important news.

429. **Revolutionary realism**, a unique form of literature, was born from the revolution, documenting the struggles of the Mexican people.

430. **Muralism, a new form of art, emerged**, visually representing the struggles of the Mexican people.
431. **Liberalism, socialism, and anarchism were major influences in the Mexican Revolution.**
432. **The Mexican Revolution** stimulated industrialization in the country due to the government's efforts to modernize the nation.
433. Partly due to the call for change in Mexico during the revolution, **education became more available to the populace,** with the government seeking to provide educational opportunities to all citizens.
434. **Political parties proliferated, as the government sought to create a more democratic system.**

435. All of **the major revolutionary leaders were killed during the war** or not long after, sometimes by former allies.
436. **Over two million people died during the violence of the Mexican revolutionary period.**
437. **The heroes of the revolution are still revered in Mexico**, with their images present in open spaces such as parks and squares.

438. **The Mexican Revolution attracted foreign mercenaries who joined various factions in the conflict.** Notably, the Irish-born American mercenary Ambrose Bierce fought **alongside Pancho Villa's** forces for a brief period. Bierce, a renowned writer, disappeared in Mexico in 1913 under mysterious circumstances.

439. **The Mexican Revolution** witnessed the implementation of unconventional warfare tactics. One notable example is the **"Zapatista War Train,"** a mobile armored train used by **Emiliano Zapata's** forces. This train was equipped with heavy artillery and allowed for rapid movement and surprise attacks against federal troops.

440. **Many women participated as soldiers, spies, nurses, and even commanders**. Some notable examples include **Carmen Serdán**, who played a key role in **the Puebla uprising**, and **Petra Herrera**, a skilled soldier who fought while being disguised as a man.

The Cristero War
(1926–1929)

> The changes brought about by **the Mexican Revolution Church** sparked a rebellion that would shake the foundations of the country. In this chapter, learn **how the rebels employed a variety of tactics against the forces of the Mexican government**. Also, discover the answer as to why the **Cristeros** rose up.

441. **During President Plutarco Elías Calles's regime, a faction of Mexican Catholics called Cristeros erupted into rebellion, triggering the Cristero War.**

442. During the uprising, **the Cristeros** adopted the slogan **of "Viva Cristo Rey"** ("Long Live Christ the King!").

443. **Most of the fighting and uprisings took place near Mexico City** and the center of the country, though the south and the eastern Baja coast were affected too. The northern part of Mexico remained relatively free of violence.

444. After **the Mexican Revolution**, Mexican authorities attempted to remove the influence of the clergy from government, especially local government, by passing laws restricting clergymen from holding public office.

445. **The Cristeros utilized a network of underground churches and priests to continue their services and rituals.**

446. **Calles's government attempted to create a secular government in which no religious organization held power and influence,** which is the main reason the Cristero movement began.

447. In response to the rebels, **the Mexican government** deployed its army to subdue the revolt.

448. **Wealthy landowners supplied the rebels with weapons and supplies.**

449. **The Catholic Church** offered assistance to the Cristeros by giving them funds and supplies.

450. **The Cristeros conducted successful ambushes against government troops.**

451. Atrocities occurred on both sides. For instance, a priest named **José Reyes Vega** doused **a train car with gasoline and set it on fire** because his younger brother had been killed. Fifty-one civilians died.

452. To garner public support, **the Cristeros held rallies and mass protests.**

453. Foreign powers, such as **the United States and Spain, sent aid to different sides during the war.**

454. **The Cristeros employed propaganda to spread their message** and appeal to the public.

455. As a symbol of their cause, **the Cristeros adopted a red flag with a white cross.**

456. To keep their operations a secret, **the Cristeros recruited female spies** disguised as vendors and travelers to gather information and smuggle guns and ammunition.

457. Many **Mexican Catholics**, as well as some **non-Catholics, provided support to the Cristeros and their cause.**

458. **The Mexican government employed various tactics to defeat the Cristeros,** such as burning villages and executing suspected rebels.

459. **The Mexican government resorted to harsh tactics, such as torture and public executions,** to try and intimidate the Cristeros into surrendering.

460. **To defeat the Cristeros, the Mexican government utilized air power to bomb the Cristero strongholds.** The pilots were reportedly American WWI veterans.

461. **In 1929, the Cristeros were defeated by the Mexican government.**

462. As a consequence of their defeat, **the Cristero War's leaders were either imprisoned or executed.**

463. **In the end, an estimated ninety thousand people perished in the Cristeros War.**

464. Following the Cristeros' defeat, **the Mexican government continued to monitor the Catholic Church** to prevent it from wielding political power.

465. Though most of **the Cristeros were motivated by religious reasons**, many others who joined the rebellion were poorer farmers and people of mixed Spanish and native backgrounds. These people fought for land reform, which came slowly and is still an issue in the country.

History of Mexico

Institutional Revolutionary Party Era
(1929–2000)

For over seven decades, **Mexico experienced a period of authoritarian rule under the** *Partido Revolucionario Institucional* **(PRI)**. A lot happened during this era, such as the monopolization of the media, economic expansion, and a high degree of patronage and corruption. Let's dive in to discover more about this influential period!

466. During this prolonged period of authoritarian rule, the Mexican government monopolized the media, broadcasting only approved messages.

467. A formidable **political machine based on patronage and bribes was established.**

468. **Patronage was utilized to ensure loyalty among public servants.**

469. While economic expansion in the form of large industries like oil and steel occurred, the majority of **the wealth was disproportionately allocated to a small group of elites.**

470. **The PRI maintained its control of power for over seven decades**, partly through electoral manipulation.

471. **Notorious for their opulence, PRI leaders were known to lead lives of luxury and host grandiose celebrations.**

472. **Mexico was heavily reliant upon external investment and loans from the United States** during this time period.

473. **Powerful drug cartels were formed during the rule of the PRI.** Many PRI officials were "on the take."

474. **Corruption and favoritism within the government were rampant.**

475. The emergence of **the Mexican labor movement,** which was committed to the defense of worker rights and social justice, happened during the PRI era.

476. **Some social and economic reforms were introduced to improve the quality of life for Mexicans.**

477. **The military was utilized to oppress political opponents.**

478. **Land reforms were implemented** to redistribute wealth to the poorest citizens, but they were few and far between. Corruption also weakened their effect.

479. **Censorship and propaganda were employed to manage public opinion.**

480. **The Catholic Church** reemerged as a powerful entity.

481. **Unions and political parties sought to eliminate the PRI's monopoly,** but they developed slowly.

482. **The Mexican border was militarized to deter illegal immigration.**

483. During the reign of the PRI, a powerful intelligence agency called the **"Dirección Federal de Seguridad,"** the **"Federal Security Directorate,"** or **"DFS,"** was created to monitor dissident groups.

484. **Political factions intended to challenge government control arose during the PRI era.**

485. **Indigenous rights groups**, hoping to oppose government policies, gained traction during this era.

486. **Highly influential business interests impacted much of Mexico's social, economic, and political life.** Businesses engaged in corruption, intimidation, and bribery.

487. In the 1980s, **Mexican drug cartels** served as conduits for the huge South American cocaine trade.

488. **Most of the leading PRI officials were from the criollo or Caucasian minority,** adding ethnic tension to Mexican social and political life.

489. **The use of torture and human rights abuses against political dissidents was commonplace.**

490. Though the Mexican government worked to keep its distance from US policies in Latin America and often opposed them, it did occasionally support US efforts in the region. For instance, **Mexico supported the US-led invasion of Panama in 1989.**

491. **Women's rights groups challenged traditional gender roles in this period.** It took time for these groups to achieve substantial progress.

History of Mexico

492. Student organizations sought to oppose government policies. One protest in particular, **the deadly Tlatelolco massacre**, marked the beginning of the PRI's slow decline.

493. **Environmental organizations striving to protect the environment were founded** in the PRI Era.

494. **Peasant organizations dedicated to the betterment of rural Mexicans were established** during this period, but the period of PRI rule is known for the party's favoritism toward the rich and powerful.

495. **Economic nationalism** was employed to protect domestic industries during this era.

496. **Trade unions that were committed to improving wages and working conditions developed.** Most unions were secretly monitored by the government.

497. **Electoral fraud was a big problem in PRI Mexico**, drawing condemnation from the US and others.

498. **In the 1970s, the Mexican economy went through many crises**, lowering the standard of living for most Mexicans. The decline of the PRI slowly began during this decade.

499. **A clandestine network of prisons was maintained to detain political dissidents.**

500. From the 1960s to the 1980s, successive PRI governments waged what is called the **"Mexican Dirty War"** on anyone who opposed them. The main target of the PRI were peasants and other reformers who were believed to be influenced by communism.

Mexican Oil Expropriation
(1938)

> When President Lázaro Cárdenas declared the Mexican oil expropriation of 1938, it sent shockwaves throughout the energy production industry and was met with vehement opposition from foreign oil companies. Undeterred by the backlash, **the Mexican government pursued the nationalization of natural resources** and embarked on a journey to create a financially independent nation. Let's uncover the controversy behind such a decision.

501. **In 1938, the Mexican government sent shockwaves throughout the world, especially the United States, when it nationalized oil and mineral production in the country.**

502. **The Mexican government** kicked out many foreign, mostly **American, oil companies that had invested millions in Mexico.**

503. **President Lázaro Cárdenas was undeterred by the backlash and vigorously pursued the nationalization of natural resources**, prompting boycotts and economic sanctions from other countries.

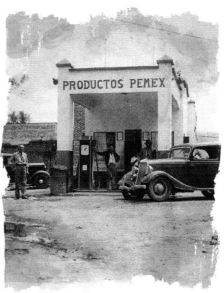

504. One definition of expropriation is **"the act of dispossessing an owner, either wholly or to a limited extent, of his property or proprietary rights."** Despite the international pressure, the Mexican government remained committed to expropriation and strove to create a financially independent nation.

505. **The Mexican oil expropriation of 1938 actually led to an increase in foreign investment** since countries were eager to invest in the newly nationalized oil industry.

506. To ensure the legality of the expropriation, **the Mexican government had to negotiate settlements with the displaced foreign oil companies**, which was a lengthy and complex endeavor.

507. Before WWII broke out, **negotiations between Mexico and foreign oil companies** led to Mexico compensating them for its takeover.

508. For the policy to be successful, **the government had to invest** significantly in the construction and operation of pipelines, refineries, storage facilities, and the new national oil company, **Petróleos Mexicanos** (Pemex).

509. **The expropriation of oil was a catalyst for economic growth and exports** but also led to criticism that the government was squandering the nation's resources and disregarding oil quality and the environment in pursuit of quantity.

510. Furthermore, **the expropriation of oil has been accused of being politically motivated** and of exacerbating inequality, leading to a debate that has surrounded it for decades.

511. For its new energy policies to reach their full potential, **the Mexican government had to pour in a great amount of investment for the development and maintenance of newly built infrastructure.** This money came from other programs, including help for the lower classes in Mexico.

512. **The United States worried that the Mexican nationalization of the oil industry** might be a first step to socialism or even communism.

513. In 1952, the Mexican government commissioned the statue and fountain called **the Fountain of Mexican Petroleum,** which was erected on a main boulevard in Mexico City.

514. When the policy was implemented, **Mexico witnessed a period of economic success and prosperity**, with oil exports becoming a major source of the government's revenue.

515. Still, **the oil industry was highly regulated by the government**, with production quotas, prices, and taxes all managed by the state.

516. **The Mexican government kept gas prices in Mexico low**, which was popular with the people.

517. In 2022, **Mexico ranked twelfth in oil production**, pumping 1.7 million barrels a day.

518. The president of Mexico during the expropriation was **Lázaro Cárdenas del Rio**, who was in office from 1934 to 1940.

519. **The expropriation of 1938 remains an iconic moment in Mexico's history**, especially since the United States was against it and interfered in Mexican politics to prevent or change the policy through boycotts, bribery, and other forms of intimidation.

520. **The oil expropriation also initiated a wave of nationalization in Mexico,** with the government taking control of other industries, such as electricity, telecommunications, banking, and railways.

521. Initially, **the United States, Great Britain, and the Netherlands boycotted all other Mexican goods as a reaction to the loss of their interests in Mexico.** The boycott ended with negotiations when WWII started.

522. **The nationalization of oil** that occurred in 1938 has been credited with providing a spark of inspiration to other Latin American countries, consequently leading to the rise of similar policies.

523. **Despite the success of oil expropriation,** the policy was and is considered highly controversial by some, with arguments questioning whether the government should have allowed foreign companies to continue to carry out operations in the country.

524. **The oil expropriation of 1938 has been credited with increasing national wealth** and helping to reduce inequality to a small degree.

525. Its detractors contend that it stifled competition and created an inefficient, **state-run oil industry.**

526. **The oil expropriation also increased government control** of the most important resource in the country.

527. The policy has also been accused of allowing **the government to become too reliant on oil revenues** to the detriment of other areas of the economy, resulting in economic stagnation and dependence on energy exports.

528. **The environmental impact of the oil expropriation has been subject to criticism,** with the production and development of the industry being blamed for pollution and the destruction of natural resources.

529. Furthermore, **many criticized the PRI for the move,** which they believed was politically motivated. The government was accused of using it to gain popular support and consolidate its power.

530. Despite its successes, **the oil expropriation of 1938 has been derided for its lack of transparency and its failure to benefit the population,** serving as a reminder that the power of nationalization should be carefully considered and applied.

Bracero Program
(1942–1964)

What began as an effort to meet the labor needs of American farmers during World War II, the Bracero (meaning "manual laborer") Program quickly spiraled into a complex web of labor rights violations, wage theft, and unjust treatment. The Bracero Program had a long-term impact on the Mexican economy, labor market, and demographics, resulting in **the permanent migration of millions of Mexicans to the United States**. Let's take a look at several important facts about this program.

531. **The Bracero Program was a series of bilateral labor agreements between the United States and Mexico.**

532. Contrary to popular belief, **the Bracero Program** was not originally intended to be a long-term arrangement.

533. **The Bracero Program was established in 1942 to meet the labor needs of American farmers** who were fighting in World War II.

534. **Mexican citizens were recruited to work in US fields**, primarily in California, Arizona, and Texas.

535. **Braceros were required to sign a contract.**

536. **They were supposed to be supplied with transportation, medical care, and housing**, although this did not always happen.

537. **The contracts were often written in English and Spanish**, with the Spanish versions often containing fewer rights than the English versions. Thus, many non-English speaking workers were not aware of their rights in the US.

538. **Penalties for contract violations included deportation and fines.**

539. **Deportations and fines** could also result from unscrupulous and/or racist farm owners.

540. **Brutal working conditions, low wages, and inadequate housing** were common for Braceros.

541. **The Bracero Program ended in 1964** and was plagued by labor rights violations and other issues.

542. According to the Pew Research Center, **the Bracero Program issued over 4.6 million contracts to Mexican workers** over its 22-year run.

543. **The US government estimated that Braceros earned an average of one dollar per hour,** which was below the federal minimum wage (which began in 1938).

544. **It is estimated that between $500 million and $1.5 billion of Bracero wages were never paid.**

545. In 1998, a settlement was agreed upon that allowed many **surviving Braceros to be paid lost wages.** In 2019, there were still thirty-six thousand Braceros awaiting payment of the settlement money.

546. **The settlement only applied to those Braceros who lived in the United States.**

547. In 2001, **several former Braceros filed a class-action suit in a federal court against the governments of the United States and Mexico**, three Mexican banks, and Wells Fargo Bank. The federal judge dismissed the lawsuit in 2002, citing expired statutes of limitations and sovereign immunity.

548. In some cases, **Braceros were forced to pay kickbacks** (bribes) to hire agents to secure employment.

549. Upon the program's termination, **many Braceros were deported** and unable to access the wages they had earned.

550. **The Bracero Program had a long-term impact on the Mexican economy** and labor market. For instance, Mexico sought to benefit from Braceros sending money back home to relatives. They also hoped that new agricultural techniques from the US would be learned.

551. **The program had a significant impact on the demography of the US-Mexico border region.**

552. It is estimated that **the Bracero Program resulted in the permanent migration** of many Mexicans to the United States.

553. According to the Migration Policy Institute, **the Bracero Program led to a decrease in the number of unauthorized Mexican immigrants in the US** since the program provided a legal and regulated way for Mexicans to enter the US.

554. **Many Mexican workers came to the US illegally** to avoid the bribes that were often necessary to enroll in the program in Mexico.

555. **The program's termination in 1964 led to a dramatic decrease in wages and working conditions for Mexican farm workers in the United States.** This was one of the main issues that led to the United Farm Workers of America, a union that was founded in the 1960s.

556. **The termination of the Bracero Program** had a limited impact on the flow of undocumented migrants crossing the US-Mexico border since the number of unauthorized immigrants had already been declining prior to the program's end in 1964.

557. **The legacy of the Bracero Program** continues to shape the debate over immigration reform in the United States.

558. **The US took 10 percent of Braceros' pay, sending it to Mexico** to be held for them when they returned, but most of them were never repaid.

559. **Many Braceros were checked for venereal diseases** when they entered the United States, which most found demeaning in the extreme.

560. The program is credited with forging stronger cultural and **economic ties between the United States and Mexico.**

561. **The Bracero Program led to the emergence of a new generation of Mexican-American families.**

562. **The program also created a new class of legal immigrants** known as legal aliens or non-citizens.

563. **The Bracero Program had a profound impact** on the lives of millions of people in the United States and Mexico.

564. **The program led to the creation of an extensive network of recruiters, labor contractors, and brokers** who continue to operate in the US and Mexico today.

565. **The Bracero Program** expanded the scope of immigration enforcement in the United States, leading to the development of more stringent immigration laws.

566. **The program led to the development of a new type of employer-sanctioned immigration,** whereby employers were able to hire foreign workers on a temporary basis.

567. **The Bracero Program** also had an effect on the language spoken in **the US-Mexico border region,** leading to the emergence of a new hybrid Spanish-English language.

568. In 1954, a major labor dispute known as **the Bracero Strike occurred in California.** Thousands of Braceros went on strike to protest against low wages and poor treatment, demanding better conditions and higher pay.

569. **The program was criticized by various civil rights organizations,** labor unions, and activists who argued that it exploited and marginalized Mexican workers and undercut wages and job opportunities for American workers.

570. **The Bracero Program officially ended on December 31st, 1964,** after years of controversy and criticism. However, its legacy continues to shape discussions on immigration, labor rights, and the relationship between the United States and Mexico.

Student Movement of 1968

On October 2nd, 1968, a significant event in Mexican history was set in motion. **A group of student activists organized a demonstration of thousands of people from all walks of life.** They were determined to challenge the oppressive rule of the Mexican government and **promote social and economic reform**. What happened during this **momentous protest**? Discover what happened to the students and why the movement is remembered as a pivotal moment in **Mexican history**.

571. **The protest known as the Mexican Student Movement or the Movement of 1968 was planned by a group of student activists.**

572. **In the months leading up to the October 2nd march in Mexico City,** clandestine meetings between **students and teachers occurred to plan the demonstration.**

573. **The march on October 2nd was planned to coincide with the start of the 1968 Olympic festivities in Mexico City** and drew international attention to Mexico.

574. **The student movement** was seen as a catalyst for a broader movement of social change in the country.

575. **The student movement led to the formation of the National Strike Council,** a coalition of student, labor, and peasant organizations.

576. **The event was sparked by the government's decision to increase fees and enforce stricter regulations on student organizations.**

577. **Pamphlets were distributed throughout Mexico City** prior to the protest to gain backing and publicize the cause.

578. **On October 2nd, 1968, the culmination of the protest was reached, with thousands of students congregating on the Zócalo, the main square in Mexico City,** and then marching through downtown Mexico City.

579. **Other demonstrations took place in cities around the country at the same time.**

580. **An estimated half a million people filled the streets** of Mexico City for the protests.

581. **The Mexican government's response to the protests** was a heavy-handed one, sending in the military to quell the demonstrations and arresting participants.

582. **The protest at Tlatelolco Plaza in Mexico City** was met with fierce police and military response.

583. **More than seven hundred people were killed**, and thousands were detained during and after the protest.

584. **The protest consisted primarily of peaceful strategies, including sit-ins and marches**, but there had been violence between rival groups of students. The government used this fact to endorse a violent crackdown supposedly on crime and communists.

585. **The government heavily censored the news**, preventing any coverage of the event. Still, word got out. Despite this, the Olympic Games were still held in Mexico City.

586. **The Mexican government used extreme measures**, such as beatings, torture, and imprisonment, to suppress protests throughout the country, although these measures were mainly used in Mexico City.

587. **The government's severe reaction to the protests resulted in public outrage**, but fear of the government and police kept many people silent.

588. **In the aftermath of the movement, the government passed laws that increased the power of the military and police in Mexico.**

589. **The movement had an influence on the 1968 Summer Olympics in Mexico City**, with the government imposing a curfew on the entire city.

590. **After the protest, some students were expelled**. Some were arrested and imprisoned.

591. **In the aftermath of the protest, many in Mexico**, including students in Mexico City and elsewhere, demanded the release of those arrested on October 2nd. Most of them were released.

592. **The protests of 1968 brought no immediate change to the Mexican government,** but the legacy of October 2nd inspired later student and civic movements, which helped break the PRI's hold on power many years later.

593. **The Student Movement of 1968 inspired other student protests globally** in a year that saw protests almost every day on a variety of issues, from human rights to the war in Vietnam.

594. **The movement gained significance as a symbol of resistance to the government's oppressive rule in Mexican history.**

595. **Mexican youths were heavily influenced by the student movements in France and the US,** which were reaching their peak at this time.

596. **The Mexico City Movement** of 1968 is regarded as the first organized student movement in Mexico.

597. **Although the protest failed to bring about its political aims, the event had a lasting impact on Mexican society**, with many of the participants later becoming influential figures in politics and business.

598. **Octavio Paz, Nobel Prize-winning author and ambassador to India, was one of many Mexican intellectuals who supported the Student Movement of 1968.**

599. The legacy of the movement is still carried on today by organizations like **the National Union of Students.**

600. Increased public awareness of the need for **a more democratic Mexico was one of the outcomes of the protests**, eventually leading to the formation of new political parties and movements.

Mexican Debt Crisis
(1982–1988)

> **In 1982, Mexico's foreign debt dramatically increased, sparking a crisis of extraordinary proportions.** Let's explore the consequences of **the Mexican debt crisis** and the steps the Mexican government took to address it. You may find yourself surprised by many of the following facts!

601. **In 1982, Mexico's foreign debt dramatically increased from $80 billion to $107 billion!**

602. **This crisis was exacerbated by over-borrowing,** skyrocketing inflation, and a weakened peso.

603. **In response, the IMF and World Bank provided Mexico with loans to stave off a total financial disaster.**

604. **Austerity plans were created by the government to help.** Reducing spending and raising taxes were the plans' main components.

605. **The Mexican debt crisis kept rising, culminating in a 1985** moratorium on repayment of foreign debt and the introduction of the nuevo peso at half the value of the old peso, which only increased inflation.

606. **The currency reform initially stabilized the economy** but caused a drastic devaluation of the peso in the global market.

607. **The peso was devalued by a staggering 80 percent!**

608. **The president of Mexico** throughout the crisis was **Miguel de la Madrid.**

609. **In 1985, a huge earthquake struck the country, further damaging the economy.** The president was booed almost everywhere he went because of his slow response to these crises.

610. **Countries like the US and Japan provided financial aid to Mexico during the crisis.**

611. This crisis was part of **the larger Latin American debt crisis,** which impacted many countries during the 1980s.

612. **The US response was lukewarm, mainly because Mexico had a history of defaulting on debt.** The US was wary of committing funds to a potentially bad investment.

613. **The crisis caused a massive capital flight from Mexico,** with foreign investment in the country declining by nearly 90 percent between 1982 and 1988.

614. **The crisis had a devastating effect on the Mexican economy**, leading to a decrease in economic growth and investment.

615. **The crisis also reduced the power and influence of the PRI** (Institutional Revolutionary Party), which was held responsible for the crisis.

616. To address the crisis, **the Mexican government introduced a series of reforms,** including the liberalization of the economy and the privatization of many state-owned companies. Pemex, the largest company in Mexico, would not become privatized.

617. To reduce its debt burden, **Mexico also implemented debt consolidation and payment rescheduling.**

618. **The overvaluation of the peso made it difficult for Mexico to export goods**, exacerbating the crisis.

619. In 1988, **Mexico was able to renegotiate its debt and obtain new loans** from international lenders, finally overcoming the crisis.

620. **Despite the crisis, Mexico still maintained a positive trade balance**, with exports rising by 35.5 percent between 1982 and 1988.

621. In 1988, **Mexico completed an agreement with its foreign debtors** that allowed it to reschedule its debt and reduce its payments by more than 70 percent.

622. In 1989, **Mexico initiated a debt-reduction program**, allowing the country to decrease its debt by $10 billion over four years.

623. **The crisis had a long-lasting effect on the Mexican economy**, with the country's GDP dropping by almost 8 percent between 1982 and 1988.

624. The crisis had a major effect on Mexico's international relations, straining the country's relationship with the US and other major creditors.

625. Because of the crisis, **Mexico adopted a more independent stance from the US** and other major creditors.

626. **Mass protests and strikes occurred in Mexico during this crisis**. Many people believed the end of PRI rule was coming, though it took about another twenty years for the party to lose control of the federal government completely.

627. To improve fiscal management, **the Mexican government adopted fiscal reforms**, such as the fiscal responsibility law, which, among other things, called for a balanced national budget. This did not happen, at least not in the way the law had planned.

628. **The crisis brought about significant changes to the Mexican financial sector**, making it more competitive and efficient.

629. **The crisis also had a negative impact on the country's balance of payments**, leading to an account deficit in 1986.

630. By 1989, **Mexico and the US were talking about a free trade agreement between them to stabilize the Mexican economy** and reduce illegal immigration to the US.

Cultural Revitalization Movement
(1980–Present)

Since the 1980s, **Mexico has been undergoing cultural revitalization, a movement that has been embraced by President López Obrador**. With an investment of more than $1.6 billion, **this movement aims to preserve and promote Mexico's indigenous languages, cultures, and traditions.** So far, efforts have resulted in tremendous changes in Mexican culture. Let's find out more about these changes in this chapter.

631. **Mexico's cultural revitalization movement began in the 1980s.**
632. The main goal of this movement is to **preserve and promote the country's indigenous languages, cultures, and traditions** after centuries of neglect or suppression.
633. Today, **over twenty-three million people in Mexico identify as indigenous**. That is almost 20 percent of the population!
634. **The foundation of the National Institute of Indigenous Languages** (INALI) in 2003 has contributed greatly to a sense of nationalism and unity in Mexico.
635. **The Mexican Secretariat of Culture** was founded in 1988 as the National Council for Culture and Arts to promote and protect Mexican art and museums.

636. In the later years of the 20th century, the works **of Mexican artists like Diego Rivera** (1886–1957) and **Frida Kahlo** (1907–1954) began to garner international attention.
637. **Cultural revitalization has led to the creation of over one hundred community radio stations around the country.** These stations are dedicated to broadcasting in the many indigenous languages of Mexico.
638. **Mexico is now home to over twelve million speakers of indigenous languages**, with a majority speaking Nahuatl, the language of the Aztecs (sometimes known as the Mexica), who dominated central Mexico during the pre-Columbian era.
639. **Spanish is the Mexican government's official language.** However, it recognizes sixty-eight languages, sixty-three of which are indigenous languages.

640. **The National Language** Plan created by **the Mexican government** implemented several initiatives to protect and promote the country's **indigenous languages.**

641. **The movement also encourages the development of educational materials in indigenous languages,** including textbooks, dictionaries, and audio-visual materials.

642. **The movement has seen the revival of traditional cultural practices,** such as the **Maya ball game**, which was banned by the Spanish in the 16th century. **Reenactors and enthusiasts often play a game** thought to be very similar to what the ancient Maya played.

643. **The movement has also seen the emergence of new cultural forms**, such as rap and hip-hop, which are performed in indigenous languages and in the majority language, Spanish.

644. It has also led to the creation of numerous indigenous-led organizations, such as **the National Indigenous Congress and the National Commission for the Development of Indigenous Peoples.**

645. **The movement gradually led to an increase in political participation by indigenous people,** with the election of several indigenous representatives to municipal and state posts and a smaller number of federal posts.

646. Many several successful films, such as **Roma** (directed by **Alfonso Cuarón**), explore **the struggles of indigenous people in Mexico.**

647. In recent years, numerous museums and cultural centers have become dedicated to preserving the country's indigenous heritage, such as **the Wixárika Cultural Center in Jalisco.**

648. **There has also been a revival of traditional crafts, such as weaving, pottery, and wood carving,** which are sold in markets and galleries around the world.

649. **Indigenous movements have not always been peaceful, such as the Zapatista Army of National Liberation,** which is dedicated to preserving the rights of indigenous people.

650. **The Zapatistas, a leftist organization, have been fighting a guerrilla war against the Mexican government since 1994.** They seek indigenous control over local resources, especially land.

651. **The movement has also seen the revival of traditional musical forms, such as mariachi and son jarocho**, which are now performed in public spaces around the country.

652. The movement led to the establishment of numerous festivals and events, such as **the Festival de la Primavera Indígena, which celebrates indigenous cultures.**

653. Literary works, such as **the novels of Elena Poniatowska** (who was wounded in the Tlatelolco Massacre), explore the lives of indigenous people in Mexico.

654. The movement saw the creation of **the National Network of Indigenous Women**, which is dedicated to defending the rights of women.

655. A new generation of filmmakers has emerged. People like **Natalia Beristáin** are dedicated to telling the stories of **indigenous people in Mexico**.

656. Numerous indigenous-controlled schools, such as **the Escuela de la Tierra**, have been established and are dedicated to **teaching students indigenous languages.**

657. Mexico has also seen the emergence of new political movements, such as **the Indigenous Rights Movement,** which is dedicated to protecting the rights of indigenous people.

658. The movement influenced education policies, leading to the inclusion of indigenous history and culture in school curricula. **Efforts were made to promote cultural diversity and respect for indigenous knowledge systems** within educational institutions.

659. **Traditional indigenous arts and crafts experienced a resurgence during the cultural revitalization movement.** Artists and artisans sought to revive traditional techniques and motifs, creating a market for indigenous artwork within Mexico and internationally.

660. **Indigenous dances and music were revitalized and incorporated into public celebrations and cultural events.** Traditional ceremonies, such as **the Day of the Dead** and other **pre-Hispanic rituals**, gained renewed popularity and became **important elements of Mexican cultural identity**.

Mexico City Earthquake
(1985)

In 1985, an 8.0 magnitude earthquake struck Mexico City. The giant tremor resulted in a large death toll and billions of dollars in destruction and struck fear in the hearts of the city's inhabitants. **Learn how this terrible tragedy affected the global economy and how Mexico rebuilt itself** from the rubble of this history-changing event.

661. On **September 19th, 1985**, a seismic event of unprecedented magnitude, estimated at **8.0, wreaked havoc on Mexico City.**
662. **The earthquake caused a death toll of five thousand to ten thousand.**
663. **The earthquake caused an estimated $5 billion in destruction.**
664. **The quake's epicenter** was located nearly two hundred miles southwest of the city.
665. **The tremor's reverberations spread across the Pacific Ocean.**
666. **The capital's** dense population and inadequate building code contributed to the number of fatalities.
667. **In the city itself, nearly four thousand structures were either destroyed or heavily damaged.**

668. The force of the quake was so strong that it **was felt as far away as Houston and Los Angeles!**
669. **After the main quake, numerous aftershocks**, some as powerful as 7.0, were felt.
670. **The disaster had ramifications in other Mexican cities**, including Guadalajara, Monterrey, and Puebla.

671. **In the capital, many government structures were either totally or partially demolished.**
672. **The quake caused serious harm to Mexico City's** public transportation system.

673. In the northern part of the city, **two huge apartment complexes were almost completely destroyed.**

674. Altogether, **Mexico City lost thirty thousand living spaces**, resulting in widespread homelessness.

675. Calculations suggest that **more than twenty thousand individuals were injured** because of the earthquake.

676. In certain parts of Mexico City, **the power blackout lasted a few days.**

677. Initially, about **two thousand soldiers and militiamen were sent into the streets** of the city to prevent looting and search for victims.

678. **Several ancient Aztec ruins were damaged by the tremor.**

679. **In the suburb of San Angel**, the seismic activity set off a massive fire injuring six hundred people.

680. In response, **Mexico City's government created a fund to provide aid to earthquake victims.**

681. **Numerous gas leaks and explosions were reported** in the aftermath of the disaster.

682. **The rupture of several major pipelines resulted in serious environmental damage.**

683. In the wake of the calamity, **the Mexican government proclaimed a state of emergency.**

684. **The tremor led to the displacement of over 100,000 people.**

685. Landslides triggered by **the earthquake obstructed roads** and caused additional destruction.

686. **Rebuilding was slowed due to the widespread corruption in government** and businesses.

687. As a result of **the government's slow response to the earthquake, many people formed civic organizations,** some of which later led to new political parties.

688. **The tremors were so powerful** that they caused the ground to sink up to one meter in some parts of Mexico City.

689. To help with reconstruction, **the Mexican government provided $4 billion in financial aid,** though the ruling PRI was heavily criticized for the slowness of their response and their initial refusal to accept foreign aid, which might have cost hundreds of lives.

690. **Foreign aid arrived** when the government admitted it could not handle the rescue and rebuilding efforts. **The United States and Israel were of significant help.**

691. Many of **the city's hospitals were damaged** beyond repair due to the quake, leading to the loss of hundreds of lives.

692. **The earthquake had a significant economic impact**, with estimates indicating that the global economy was affected to the tune of $6 billion.

693. **The seismic waves of the quake** were visible on seismographs in Washington, DC.

694. **The Mexican government declared three days of national mourning** in the wake of the disaster.

695. **The earthquake was the result** of the subduction of the Cocos Plate beneath the North American plate along the Middle America Trench.

696. In the aftermath of the quake, **over thirty thousand people were made destitute.**

697. **The quake caused the water level** of the city's main lake, Texcoco, **to drop by more than three feet.**

698. In some places near Mexico City, **the earth shook for more than five minutes!** This is an extraordinarily long time for an earthquake.

699. **The tremors caused a number of landslides**, resulting in the collapse of several mountainsides and hillsides.

700. **Exactly thirty-seven years later, on September 19th, 2022, a series of earthquakes hit Mexico and Mexico City.** Though the death toll was only two people, many buildings were damaged. Many people who had lived through the 1985 earthquake thought another "big one" might be coming.

North American Free Trade Agreement (NAFTA) (1994)

The North American Free Trade Agreement (NAFTA) was signed in 1992 and enacted two years later. **The purpose of the deal was to reduce trade barriers between the countries,** and it certainly achieved that goal. However, **NAFTA has also been denounced for possibly causing the displacement of workers** in specific industries and infringing upon labor rights and ecological regulations. Let's dig into this historic agreement!

701. At the time **the North American Free Trade Agreement (NAFTA) was signed in 1992, it was the biggest free trade agreement in the world.**

702. **NAFTA involved Canada, the US, and Mexico.**

703. **The agreement included** provisions for environmental and labor regulations.

704. The principal purpose of NAFTA was **to diminish tariffs and other trade impediments between the countries.**

705. Subsequently, **the amount of trade between the three nations** skyrocketed to more than $1.2 trillion in 2018 from $297 billion in 1993.

706. **In Mexico and Canada, NAFTA has been credited with promoting productivity,** job creation, and higher wages, thereby leading to improved living standards.

707. **The treaty abolished most taxes on goods traded between the countries** and ended non-tariff barriers, such as quotas.

708. **The agreement also set up methods for resolving disputes** between the signatories.

709. In addition, **NAFTA created the North American Development Bank**, which gives grants and loans for economic and social development projects in Mexico and the US.

710. **NAFTA has also been denounced for possibly causing the displacement of workers** in certain industries and infringing upon individual national labor rights and ecological regulations.

711. **Due to the structure of NAFTA**, which took years to negotiate and pass, there were very few ways to enforce violations of the agreement.

712. Despite this, **NAFTA has been credited with pulling Mexico from economic stagnation and many Mexicans from poverty**, creating millions of jobs in the US, Mexico, and Canada, as well as diminishing the cost of consumer goods in all three countries.

713. The agreement also gave birth to **the North American Leaders' Summit**, which meets yearly to address economic and security matters. This meeting of the leaders of Mexico, the US, and Canada is often referred to as **the "Three Amigos Summit"** in the press.

714. **NAFTA contributed to improved relations between the US and Mexico.**

715. **NAFTA was the first free trade agreement to feature a dispute resolution** mechanism, allowing signatories to settle disagreements without going to court.

716. It was also credited with **reducing poverty and inequality in Mexico and raising the quality of goods produced** in all three nations.

717. **It has been criticized for its lack of provisions for the protection of intellectual property rights and labor rights.**

718. Although **President Bill Clinton is often credited with the creation of NAFTA**, negotiations began during the Reagan administration.

719. **NAFTA brought about enhanced efficiency and cost savings** in the production of many goods, such as automobiles.

720. **It has also been credited with decreasing the expense of cross-border investments.**

721. **The agreement is said to have assisted in decreasing Mexico's reliance on oil exports** and making the country more competitive in manufacturing and service industries.

722. **NAFTA has been credited with improving access to markets in all three countries** and lowering corruption in some parts of the Mexican economy.

723. **It also leveled the playing field for small- and medium-sized businesses** in all three countries.

724. **The agreement is believed to have helped create a more unified North American energy market**, leading to greater efficiency and savings.

725. **Small-scale farms in Mexico benefited more from NAFTA than large-scale ones.** Farming was popular among many of the indigenous people of the country.

726. **NAFTA was the first free trade agreement that included provisions** for the protection of intellectual property rights.

727. Once NAFTA was implemented, the amount of **foreign direct investment in Mexico increased** greatly compared to before its introduction.

728. **The treaty has been responsible for the creation of over fourteen million jobs** in all three countries combined.

729. **NAFTA became a bone of contention in the 1994 US presidential election**. Republican candidate **Bob Dole** and independent candidate **Ross Perot** claimed NAFTA would cost the US more jobs than it created. This was somewhat true in the automobile industry.

730. Most moderate and progressive economists agree that **NAFTA was a positive for the US, Mexico, and Canada.**

731. One positive for Mexico was that despite some ups and downs, **NAFTA helped the agricultural and beef sectors** of its economy.

732. **Changes in income have led to a fundamental shift in the Mexican diet.** With a higher per capita income, the Mexican diet has begun to include more beef and less vegetables.

733. **The middle class in Mexico has grown** since the implementation of NAFTA.

734. With an exception during **the Great Recession of 2008/09**, unemployment in Mexico has trended downward since the passage of NAFTA.

735. In 2018, **NAFTA was renegotiated and replaced with the United States-Mexico-Canada Agreement** (USMCA), which began in 2020.

Formation of the Party of the Democratic Revolution (PRD)
(1989)

Since its inception in 1989, **the Party of the Democratic Revolution (PRD) has been a strong voice and major force in Mexican politics**. Walk with us as we learn about **Cuauhtémoc Cárdenas's** journey and how it marked the beginning of an unprecedented period of political turmoil in Mexico. **Let's look at how the PRD has been an important voice in Mexico's** struggle for democracy, freedom, and social justice.

736. **The PRD was founded in 1989 by Cuauhtémoc Cárdenas, the son of former President Lázaro Cárdenas** (1934–1940), and other left-wing intellectuals and activists.

737. **The party was created in response to the lack of electoral choice in Mexico** and aimed to represent a "third way" between the ruling **Institutional Revolutionary Party** (PRI) and the right-wing **National Action Party** (PAN).

738. **The PRD, which included a number of former PRI members**, was the first party to challenge the PRI's decades-long domination of Mexican politics.

739. **The PRD's founders included** academics, intellectuals, and activists, such as **Ricardo Lagos, Marcela Lombardo, and Emilio Álvarez Icaza.**

740. **The party's political platform** was based on the values of democracy, freedom, and social justice.

741. **Cárdenas was the leader of the PRD** and was elected head of government of Mexico City, a powerful position that gave the PRD a very public platform.

742. **Cárdenas was elected to the Senate in 1976** and became governor of the state of Michoacán in 1980.

743. **In 1997, the PRD had the second-largest percentage of seats in the Chamber of Deputies,** which was a remarkable rise, considering the PRI waged a campaign of intimidation, violence, and assassination against the PRD.

744. **The PRD's rise to power led to a period of intense political turmoil in Mexico** since there was an intense battle for control of the government. Many PRD supporters were jailed, killed, or "disappeared" during this time.

745. **During this time, the PRD was active in advocating for electoral reforms**, including the introduction of proportional representation, the abolition of the single-member district system, and the introduction of direct presidential elections.

746. **The PRD's influence waned in the early 2000s**, as the party became increasingly divided and was unable to agree on a unified strategy.

747. **A number of PRD officials were caught receiving bribes.**

748. In 2006, the PRD candidate **Andrés Manuel López Obrador** narrowly lost the presidential election to **Felipe Calderón of the PAN.**

749. **In 2012, the PRD again backed López Obrador**, but he lost the election to a resurgent and "changed" PRI, whose candidate was Enrique Peña Nieto.

750. **The PRD also had success at the local level,** winning numerous mayoral and state races in Mexico City and the states of Michoacán, Chiapas, Puebla, and Veracruz.

751. Though **the PRD's influence waned in the early 2000s**, it was critical in creating change in the Mexican political landscape by giving the people a reasonable alternative to the PRI.

752. **The PRD is a member of the Socialist International** and has close ties to the Mexican Workers' Party, the Ecologist Green Party of Mexico, and other leftist political organizations.

753. **The PRD was one of the first Mexican political parties to support the legalization of same-sex marriage** and the adoption of other progressive policies on social issues.

754. **The PRD has faced numerous legal challenges** over the years, including accusations

of electoral fraud and misappropriation of public funds.

755. **PRD members have also been accused of corruption** and involvement in organized crime.

756. **The party has been accused of using patronage and favoritism** to build its political base, particularly in the state of Michoacán.

757. **Corruption and financial irregularities have decreased the popularity of the PRD in recent years.**

758. **The PRD has close ties to labor unions and other social movements.** It has been active in advocating for improved labor rights for Mexican workers.

759. In recent years, **the PRD has been criticized for its perceived lack of internal democracy,** with party leaders accused of stifling debate and restricting the involvement of rank-and-file members.

760. **The party has been accused of being too closely aligned with President López Obrador** (elected in 2018), who splintered off from the PRD and created **the Morena Party** in 2018. Critics claim the party has become too "presidentialist" in its approach to politics. In other words, they believe there is too much power in the executive branch.

761. **The PRD's success has inspired the formation of numerous other parties in Mexico,** including **the Citizens' Movement, the Morena Party, and the Social Encounter Party.**

762. Since 2020, the PRD has been part of a multi-party coalition in Mexico called **"Va por Mexico,"** meaning "It's for Mexico."

763. **The party has taken steps to improve its internal organization,** introducing new rules and regulations to ensure greater transparency and accountability.

764. More recently, **the PRD has been active in the international arena,** advocating for indigenous rights and taking part in international conferences.

765. **The PRD has been a major force in Mexican politics** for more than three decades and continues to influence Mexican politics.

History of Mexico

Zapatista Uprising
(1994)

On the morning of January 1st, 1994, **Subcomandante Marcos**, known to many of his supporters as **the Masked Angel of Revolt**, became the "face" of **the Zapatista Uprising**. Let's look at this revolutionary movement and the indelible marks it left on the world.

766. **Subcomandante Marcos became the "face" of the Zapatista Uprising.** Marcos had been a brilliant student and professor of philosophy and literature at the Autonomous Metropolitan University in the 1980s before adopting revolutionary politics and moving to Chiapas in 1984.

767. **On the same day the North American Free Trade Agreement was inked, the Zapatista Uprising began.**

768. **The Zapatista Uprising was a movement to battle the exploitation of indigenous people in Mexico**, especially in rural Chiapas.

769. **The Zapatista Uprising** was one of the first political revolts covered on the internet.

770. In 1994, **the Zapatistas called for an armed uprising against the Mexican government,** but they did not garner the countrywide support they had hoped for.

771. **On the day of the protest, civic centers were attacked**, indigenous prisoners were released, and land records were destroyed.

772. **The police and army were sent to put down the uprising**. Around three hundred people were killed.

773. **The Zapatistas waged their "war" in the media** and by word of mouth, telling the world about the abuses and discrimination **indigenous people in Chiapas** and all of Mexico experienced.

774. **Though the Zapatista Uprising did not accomplish its aims**, other indigenous groups in Latin America were inspired by it.

775. Well-known people like **director Michael Moore** and philosopher and scientist **Noam Chomsky** lent their support to the Zapatista Uprising.

776. **The Zapatista Uprising played a significant role in the emergence of the "anti-globalization" movement.**

777. Films, books, and other media have chronicled **the Zapatista Uprising**, such as the movie *Zapatista* released in 1999.

778. **The movement was named in honor of Emiliano Zapata**, one of the leaders of the 1910 revolution.

779. **The Zapatistas called for land reform and less globalization**, which they saw as causing greater poverty in Chiapas and among many indigenous groups in Latin America.

780. Today, **areas of Chiapas are recognized**, even if it's unofficially, as being autonomous parts of Mexico.

781. **The Zapatista Uprising was successful in garnering international attention** for the problems of indigenous people in Mexico.

782. **Subcomandante Marcos's real name is Rafael Sebastian Guillen Vicente**, and he is still a prominent figure in Chiapas almost thirty years after the uprising began.

783. **There are a number of political parties that reflect many of the Zapatistas' core beliefs.**

784. **The Zapatistas** gained a great deal of support overseas.

785. Though **the Zapatistas** did not achieve their immediate goals, the Mexican government's failure to stop it signaled to much of Mexico that the PRI was not as strong as it had been.

786. **The Zapatista Uprising** is believed to have given rise to autonomous indigenous communities in Mexico.

787. **The Zapatista Uprising has been credited with inspiring the Intercontinental Network of Indigenous Peoples and Nations.**

788. Before the uprising, **the Zapatistas organized a group of women** that wrote what is known as **the Zapatista Women's Revolutionary Law**, which helped women participate in the movement and gain equality in decision-making.

789. In 1997, **forty-five members of a religious group associated with the Zapatistas were massacred by a right-wing paramilitary group in Acteal, a small village in Chiapas.**

790. In 2020, **the Mexican government released information linking the Secretariat of Home Affairs**, a government agency, to the massacre.

History of Mexico

Migration to the United States
(1970s–present)

For decades, the influx of Mexican immigrants to the United States has been a source of controversy and political complexity. Learn how the influx of **Mexican immigrants and immigrants from other Latin American countries** crossing the border has affected the US and Mexico. Discover how **the Trump administration stepped up immigration enforcement efforts,** and explore some facts about **Mexican immigration** under the Biden administration.

791. **In the 1970s, the estimated number of Mexican immigrants annually moving to the United States exceeded a million,** though most of those people either returned to Mexico permanently or traveled between both countries, mostly illegally.

792. **In the 1970s, Mexican immigrants were often excluded from government programs** meant to aid other immigrant groups.

793. **Most Mexican migrant workers engaged in agricultural, construction, and service** vocations in the United States from the 1970s to the 2020s.

794. In the 1970s, **the majority of Mexican immigrants living in the United States were young men** searching for work opportunities.

795. During the 1990s, **more than half of Mexican immigrants to the United States were below the age of twenty-five.**

796. The number of **Mexican immigrants to the United States** saw a growth in the 1980s and 1990s, reaching over seven million in 2000.

797. By 2017, the total number of **Mexican immigrants to the United States** had grown to about 10.5 million.

798. The estimation of **undocumented Mexican immigrants in the United States yearly is over ten million since 2000.** This number includes immigrants who become permanent or semi-permanent residents and those who migrate between the two countries.

799. Since 2000, the number of **Mexican immigrants to the United States** has grown at a slower rate than other immigrant groups from Latin America.

800. In the 2010s, **the United States experienced a downturn in Mexican immigrants** for the first time since the 1970s.

801. From 2011 to 2017, the number of **Mexican immigrants to the United States declined** by 8.4 percent.

802. **Today, most of the migrants coming to the US from Latin America are not Mexican,** but they use Mexican territory to get to US shores, which is a problem for both governments.

803. **In 2015, Mexicans made up about 55 percent of the illegal immigrant population in the US.** In that year, there were around twelve million illegal immigrants.

804. The number of **Mexican immigrants removed from the United States** in 2017 was the highest amount since 2012.

805. **The Trump administration** sought to curb legal **immigration from Mexico** through the implementation of the Remain in Mexico policy.

806. **Donald Trump's campaign promise to make Mexico pay for his planned wall** on the US-Mexico border was met with both derision and hostility in Mexico.

807. Since 2020, **the US government** has sought to reduce the number of asylum seekers from Mexico.

808. In 2021, **the Biden administration instituted policies meant to protect the rights of Mexican immigrants in the United States**.

809. **In 2021, the United States observed a substantial expansion in the number of Mexican immigrants entering the country**, with a calculated 100,000 entering from January to March. Part of the reason for this was the need for workers in the US during the 2020 pandemic.

810. In 2021, **the Biden administration aimed to expand access to legal immigration for Mexican immigrants** and to reunite families separated by deportation.

811. Despite **the U.S.-Mexico border wall's** use of the latest in fencing and surveillance technology, it is still regularly breached by criminals and migrants. The wall does not run along the entire border.

812. **As of January 2020, the wall had cost over eleven billion dollars**, and most of what was supposed to be built was not. The Biden administration halted building the wall, saying it was costly and ineffective.

813. **The border wall is divided into three sections with different types of barriers**. The **first section is a physical barrier** made of steel posts that are eighteen to thirty feet tall. **The second section is a virtual wall** made up of sensors, cameras, and radar systems. The **third section is a "virtual fence"** that uses drones, helicopters, and other aircraft to monitor the border.

814. **The construction of the wall has been met with significant opposition from Native American groups and environmentalists.**

815. **The wall has caused significant economic disruption in border towns**, including reduced tourism and disruption of traditional farming methods.

816. **The US government has used eminent domain to take land from private citizens** for the construction of the wall.

817. **The wall has caused considerable social tension**, as it divides families and communities along the border.

818. While **the wall did not reduce the number of immigrants from Latin America** to any great degree, it has changed the manner in which many people cross the border, including some very dangerous methods.

819. **The wall has been a source of political tension between the US and Mexico**, with the latter accusing the former of violating its sovereignty.

820. In addition to facing discrimination and more in **the US, immigrants from Latin America and Mexico are regularly abused and taken advantage of by drug cartels and "coyotes,"** people who specialize in beating the US Border Patrol for a large price.

National Action Party (PAN) Era
(2000–2012)

The PAN (Partido Acción Nacional) era was a transformative period in Mexico, as the country embraced unprecedented gains in technology, trade, and improvements to standards of living. Its infrastructure also saw massive investment, resulting in a wide variety of new national programs. **It is no surprise that the PAN era is remembered as a period of tremendous progress and innovation for Mexico.**

821. **In 2000, PAN leader Vicente Fox was the first non-PRI member elected president in seventy years.**

822. **The economy of Mexico grew** by an average of 3 percent annually during the PAN era.

823. **During the PAN era, Mexico began using biometric technology** to issue national identification cards to curb crime, drug smuggling, terrorism, and illegal immigration.

824. **Under PAN, Mexico signed free trade agreements with the United States, Canada, and other countries** that have proved largely beneficial.

825. **Vicente Fox proposed Plan Puebla Panama in 2001**, a joint strategy with other Central American countries to provide new superhighways along the Pacific and Gulf coasts, as well as other improvements and political agreements.

826. **PAN oversaw the completion of the Trans-Isthmus of Tehuantepec Railway, connecting the Pacific and Atlantic coasts of Mexico.** The railway is known today as the Ferrocarril Transístmico.

827. **The G20 Summit, an important meeting of the world's largest economies, was hosted by Mexico in 2012 during the Enrique Peña Nieto administration.**

828. **Under PAN, Mexico made significant progress** in reducing poverty.

829. **The party believes in minimal interference from the government in private enterprise,** concerning some in Mexico who believe corruption is still rife in the country.

830. **Despite his personal popularity, Vicente Fox** had difficulty governing because he was elected when **PAN only controlled a minority of seats in Congress.**

831. **Under PAN, Mexico launched the Program for the Strengthening of Local Governments,** giving greater autonomy to the country's municipalities.

832. During the PAN era, **many Mexicans began to form environmental protection groups.**

833. As a response to **the Zapatista** movement, **PAN encouraged and sponsored a number of indigenous peoples' groups.**

834. Under **PAN, Mexico made strides in modernizing its energy sector,** developing renewable energy sources and reducing dependence on fossil fuels.

835. **Despite opposition from PAN, abortion became legal in Mexico in 2000.**

836. **During the PAN era, Mexico made significant advances in the fight against drug trafficking and organized crime,** but there is still much work to be done.

837. **Since it lost power in 2012, PAN has been plagued with much infighting between factions.**

838. **There are two main factions within PAN today**: moderates and conservatives.

839. Some Mexicans are uncomfortable with the **close relationship between PAN and the Roman Catholic Church in Mexico.**

840. **Mexican presidents serve one six-year term**. In the 2018 presidential election, PAN came in a distant second to **the Morena Party**, with **López Obrador becoming president.**

Election of Andrés Manuel López Obrador (AMLO)
(2018)

Andrés Manuel López Obrador, commonly known as AMLO, has been a significant force in Mexican politics in recent years. From his earlier years in the student movement to his victorious campaign and election to the Mexican presidency in 2018, **AMLO has been a dedicated advocate for social welfare, democracy, and anti-corruption.** He is the leader of many firsts during his term as president. Let's look at how he has brought a new level of success to his country.

841. **Andrés Manuel López Obrador**, commonly known as **AMLO**, was born in 1953 in the Mexican state of Tabasco.

842. **He is the youngest of seven children and was raised in the small town of Macuspana.**

843. **He has been active in politics since the 1970s.**

844. **AMLO held local, state, and federal posts** before becoming president.

845. He was a founding member of **the Mexican Democratic Party** (now defunct) and has been involved in many political campaigns.

846. **From 2000 to 2005, AMLO served as the head of government (mayor) of Mexico City.**

847. While **mayor of Mexico City**, he implemented a range of social welfare projects, including **free public transportation for students and the elderly.**

848. In the early 2000s, **AMLO became a vegetarian.**

849. **He does not consume alcohol**; he has been candid about his dislike of drinking.

850. After unsuccessfully running for president twice (2006 and 2012), **he was elected in 2018 with a landslide victory.**

851. **He was the first president since 1988 to win an outright majority**. He carried thirty-one of Mexico's thirty-two states!

852. **He is known for his anti-corruption stance.**

853. **AMLO is the first president from Morena,** a left-wing political party that was founded in 2012 and focuses on advancing social welfare and promoting democracy.

854. **He is the first president in Mexican history not to come from the two major parties; for decades,** the two major parties, the PRI and PAN, held a monopoly on the Mexican presidency.

855. **AMLO is the first leftist president in Mexico in over seventy years.** The last leftist president in Mexico was Lázaro Cárdenas, who was in office from 1934 to 1940.

856. **AMLO's administration has been focused on providing social welfare programs.** He has sought to reduce inequality and increase access to services such as healthcare, education, and housing.

857. **He has instituted many policies and measures to increase his government's transparency and accountability,** though his implementation of a new transparency policy has been criticized as being "not transparent enough."

858. **His administration has implemented a number of initiatives to increase wages and reduce educational inequality,** such as raising the minimum wage and providing free tuition for public universities.

859. **He has implemented a universal pension program for the elderly**, providing a basic pension to all elderly people over the age of sixty-five, regardless of whether they were formally employed or not.

860. **He has lowered the salaries for high-ranking public officials** and instituted salary caps for these positions.

861. **He has called for a moratorium on oil drilling in the Gulf of Mexico,** taking a stand against reckless oil drilling.

862. **He has reduced tax exemptions for the wealthy and added a luxury tax on high-end items.**

863. **AMLO has increased subsidies for small farmers and rural communities,** seeking to reduce poverty in rural areas by providing subsidies for small farmers he believes have been hurt by NAFTA.

864. **He has focused on improving infrastructure throughout Mexico**, including new budgets for building new roads, bridges, and public transportation systems.

865. **His administration has been a major proponent of renewable energy sources** and has encouraged the development of solar and wind power.

866. **He has implemented a series of initiatives to reduce poverty by providing subsidies for food, housing, and education.**

867. He has increased **the focus on protecting Mexico's environment**, taking steps to reduce pollution, conserve water, and protect endangered species.

868. **He has attempted to reduce the power of drug cartels in Mexico,** taking a hard stance against organized crime and implementing measures to combat drug trafficking, but it's a tough battle that continues today.

869. **AMLO has increased public spending on healthcare** and created policies to reduce the cost of prescription drugs.

870. **López Obrador has reduced income taxes for middle- and lower-income earners** to reduce inequality.

871. **Access to clean water and sanitation**, particularly in rural areas, has been a priority.

872. **He has sought to increase access to the internet and technology for all Mexicans.**

873. **Increased access to justice and legal services** for all Mexicans is on AMLO's agenda.

874. **He has sought to protect Mexico's cultural heritage and identity**, increasing funding for cultural programs and initiatives. He has also taken steps to preserve indigenous languages and traditions.

875. **AMLO has been more focused on domestic affairs instead of foreign relations** since becoming president.

War on Drugs
(2006–present)

Mexico's war on drugs is a conflict shrouded in violence and tragedy. To combat the spread of organized crime, **the Mexican government has taken many steps**, as you'll learn below. Since this situation involves the US as well, we will also take a look at **how America has provided extensive support to the Mexican government** and extradited hundreds of drug traffickers for prosecution. As **the war on drugs continues**, learn how Mexico is increasingly relying on cutting-edge technology to bring the conflict to an end.

876. **The drug wars in Mexico** have resulted in the deaths of over seventy thousand people since the 1980s, perhaps more.

877. **Exacerbated by corruption, hundreds of police officers and politicians have been arrested or convicted for their involvement in the drug trade.**

878. **The US has offered financial, logistical, and intelligence support to the Mexican government** in its fight against organized crime. Hundreds of drug traffickers have been extradited to the US for prosecution.

879. **The Sinaloa Cartel and the Jalisco New Generation Cartel** are two of the most powerful drug cartels active in Mexico today.

880. **Hundreds of thousands of Mexican troops and police have waged a war on drugs** and drug cartels in the last few decades.

881. In addition to cocaine and other drugs, **Mexico struggles with the import, production, and trafficking of the deadly drug fentanyl.**

882. The use of **private security companies to protect businesses** and wealthy individuals from the violence of **the drug wars has become commonplace in Mexico.**

883. Despite the Mexican government's massive effort to end the drug wars, **Mexico has met widespread criticism for its failure to significantly reduce the power of drug cartels** and the skyrocketing increase in violent crime.

884. **Disappearances have risen sharply in recent years,** with many believed to be connected to organized crime and drug trafficking.

885. **The Mexican government has sought to strengthen border security** and increase the number of drug interdiction operations.

886. In 2008, **Mexican President Felipe Calderón declared a "war on drugs"** and launched a nationwide campaign against drug cartels.

887. **The US and Mexico signed a joint declaration to fight drug trafficking** and organized crime in 2011.

888. **The Mexican Navy has played an integral role in the war on drugs,** conducting several high-profile operations against drug traffickers.

889. **Mexico has established several specialized police forces to combat drug trafficking and organized crime.** These units have been chosen and carefully screened for corrupt activity, but no program is perfect.

890. **The Mexican government launched a new strategy to combat drug trafficking** in 2012, emphasizing reducing violence, increasing intelligence gathering and sharing, and strengthening international cooperation.

891. In 2014, **the US and Mexico signed a new border security agreement** that included increased information sharing and increased security along the border.

892. In 2015, **Mexico launched a new campaign to combat drug trafficking,** prioritizing the prevention of violence and the protection of human rights.

893. **Mexico embarked on a new anti-drug strategy** centered on prevention, enforcement, and alternative development programs in 2016.

894. In 2021, **Mexico legalized the recreational use of marijuana**, partly to free up police for the fight against other drugs.

895. **The Mexican government has started a number of social programs** to reduce poverty and improve public safety in areas affected by drug trafficking.

896. **Mexico has taken a hardline stance against drug traffickers,** including the use of asset forfeiture and the extradition of suspects to the US.

897. Like the DEA (**Drug Enforcement Agency**) in the US, **special law enforcement units have been created by Mexican** authorities to investigate money laundering and financial crimes related to drug trafficking.

898. In 2017, **the Mexican government launched a new strategy focusing on the disruption of drug supply networks,** improved intelligence sharing, and increased international cooperation.

899. **The Mexican government has taken steps to reduce the demand for drugs,** such as launching public awareness campaigns and implementing public health programs.

900. **Mexico has also sought to strengthen the law and reduce impunity by prosecuting high-level drug traffickers.**

901. **Mexico has deployed military forces to protect a number of key infrastructure projects,** such as oil pipelines, from drug-trafficking activities.

902. **Drug gangs essentially run many towns and cities,** especially near the US border, and have used money from the drug trade to branch out into other areas. Some of these other activities are legal, but most are illegal.

903. **Mexico has sought to increase public confidence** in the rule of law by creating an independent police oversight agency and launching an anti-corruption reform effort.

904. **Many drug dealers have been extradited to the US,** not only because of American pressure but also because **the Mexican judiciary has been affected by corruption and intimidation by the cartels.**

905. **Mexican authorities have increasingly relied on technology to combat drug trafficking,** such as drones, facial recognition software, and biometric identification systems.

Increase in Gang Violence
(2010–present)

An alarming surge in gang-related violence has struck Mexico, a problem that is affecting much of the world. While this topic is difficult to discuss, it is important to understand how this kind of violence disrupts daily life. Though the **Mexican government has responded with a number of initiatives,** experts believe more needs to be done to **tackle the root causes of the violence.** Let's consider some of the important facts surrounding this **alarming trend and the war aimed at decimating it.**

906. **Mexico has seen periods of alarming growth and occasional declines in its murder rate** since 2005. In 2020, the homicide rate was around twenty-eight people per every thousand. The US murder rate in 2020 was half that.

907. **The Mexican government estimates that there are currently over 100,000 drug gang members in Mexico,** with many more involved in other criminal activities.

908. **The majority of those gang members are under the age of twenty-five.**

909. **Drug trafficking is the main source of income for gangs in Mexico,** with the drug trade estimated to generate $19 to $29 billion annually.

910. **The two largest gangs in Mexico are the Sinaloa Cartel and the Juarez Cartel**, each concentrating on drug trafficking.

911. Other gangs **include the Gulf Cartel, the Tijuana Cartel, the Knights Templar, and the Zetas,** although some of them are no longer active.

912. **Gang members are increasingly using more deadly weapons,** such as **AK-47s** and **grenades**, to conduct their activities.

913. **Gang violence has become so severe that some Mexican cities are among the most dangerous in the world.**

914. **The border cities of Tijuana, Ciudad Juarez, and Nuevo Laredo are particularly affected by gang violence.**

915. **The Mexican government has responded to the rising violence by deploying the army** to help local police forces.

916. **The government has implemented a variety of social programs** to try to address the root causes of gang violence.

917. **The government has also tried to combat the gangs by offering rewards for information** leading to the arrest of gang leaders.

918. **The US government has been actively involved in helping Mexico fight the gangs,** providing training, equipment, and intelligence to the Mexican police and military.

919. **The Mexican government has recently begun collecting data on gang-related homicides,** but the data is incomplete and often unreliable. Not all gang violence is public. Much of it goes on behind the scenes, and most witnesses are threatened to keep quiet.

920. **The lack of reliable data on gang violence makes it difficult to measure the effectiveness of the government's efforts to combat it.**

921. **Corruption is another major problem in Mexico,** as gangs often use bribery and intimidation to avoid prosecution.

922. **Mexico's weak justice system is another factor** that has enabled gangs to operate with impunity.

923. **Poverty and inequality have been identified as major factors** driving the growth of gangs in Mexico.

924. **Gangs have been able to exploit the lack of economic opportunities in Mexico's** poorer districts and have used violence to control local markets.

925. **The violence of Mexico's gangs has had a devastating impact on the country's economy,** with some estimates suggesting that the cost of gang violence could be as high as $50 billion a year.

926. **Gangs have also been linked to the proliferation of weapons**, as they often use violence to acquire and protect their illegal arms caches.

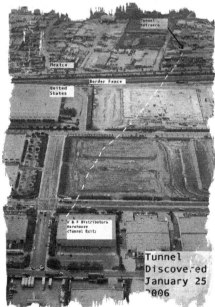

927. **The violence has led to a dramatic increase in the number of people fleeing the country,** with more than 600,000 people leaving Mexico in 2017 alone.

928. **Gang violence has had a devastating impact on Mexico's education system**, with many teachers and students fleeing the country or being forced to stay away from school due to fear of violence.

929. **The gangs have been linked to the trafficking of women and children**, as they often use them as sexual slaves or to smuggle drugs.

930. **The gangs have also been linked to the illegal mining of gold and other minerals**, as they often use violence and intimidation to control mining operations in remote areas of the country. In recent years, there have been concerns that they are taking control of the logging and fishing industries.

931. **Many fear that if the violence continues, the Mexican government could swing very right** and see the re-emergence of right-wing "death squads," which were part of the Mexican political scene in the 1970s.

932. **The government has recently implemented a number of measures aimed at tackling gang violence**, including the creation of a **National Council for Security** and a new anti-gang program.

933. **The government has implemented a series of measures aimed at improving the functioning of the justice system**, including the creation of a new federal police force and the establishment of a specialized anti-gang unit.

934. **Top secret anti-corruption units have been tasked** with rooting out bribery and intimidation by the drug cartels within the legal system and other parts of the government.

935. **Many Mexican gangs have members operating in the United States and Mexico.**

Sports in Mexico

Mexico has produced a remarkable number of sports icons who have left an indelible mark on the world stage. **From football fields to golf courses and boxing rings to racquetball courts,** these extraordinary individuals have captured the hearts of fans and exemplified the grit, talent, and determination that define **Mexican sporting prowess.**

In this section, we delve into **the fascinating world of Mexican sports icons,** uncovering thirty-two unique facts that showcase their remarkable achievements, contributions, and enduring legacies.

936. **Hugo Sánchez, known as "Hugol," is the only Mexican football** (called soccer in the US) player to have won **the Pichichi Trophy as the top scorer in La Liga.**

937. **Footballer Cuauhtémoc Blanco** was renowned for his skillful dribbling and unique playing style.

938. **Ana Gabriela Guevara won a silver medal** in the 400-meter race at the 2004 Summer Olympics in Athens.

939. **Julio César Chávez is considered by many to be one of the greatest boxers** who ever lived.

940. **Raúl González became one of the highest-scoring Spanish players** in the history of La Liga.

941. **Taekwondo athlete María Espinoza** won gold at the 2008 Olympics.

942. **Footballer Rafael Márquez** captained the Mexican national team in five World Cups and enjoyed a successful career in Europe.

943. **Fernando Valenzuela, a Mexican baseball pitcher**, enjoyed tremendous success in the US Major Leagues. He achieved the rare feat of winning both the Cy Young Award and the Rookie of the Year Award in the same season in 1981.

944. **Football goalkeeper Jorge Campos** revolutionized the position with his colorful and innovative playing style.

945. **Germán Villa Castañeda** was on two Mexican World Cup teams and is considered one of **the best Mexican footballers** of recent years.

946. **Saul "Canelo" Álvarez from Guadalajara** has been ranked as the best or one of **the best boxers in the world** for the last few years and is a superstar in Mexico today.

947. **Paola Espinosa** has won multiple Olympic medals and is considered one **of Mexico's greatest divers.** She represented Mexico at three Olympic Games: 2004, 2008, and 2012.

948. **Javier "Chicharito" Hernández, a popular football striker**, has represented Mexico in multiple World Cups and achieved success in European and American leagues. In the summer of 2023, he suffered a massive knee injury that may end his career.

949. At the Sydney 2000 Olympic Games, **Soraya Jiménez, a weightlifter**, became the first female Mexican athlete to win a gold medal.

950. **Football goalie Antonio Carbajal** holds the record for being the only player to have appeared in five consecutive World Cups (1950–1966). Carbajal passed in 2023 at the age of ninety-three.

951. **Joaquín Capilla, a diver, won four Olympic medals**, including a gold at the 1956 Melbourne Olympic Games.

952. **Salvador Sánchez, a celebrated boxer,** held the WBC (World Boxing Council) featherweight championship and had a formidable boxing record. He was killed in a car crash at the age of twenty-four in 1982.

953. **Ana María Torres, a professional boxer**, became a world champion in the super flyweight division and inspired female boxers in Mexico.

954. **Sául Hernández won first place in the 1500-meter wheelchair race** at the 2000 Olympic Games. He has won six medals in the Paralympic Games, with his career lasting from 1988 to 2008.

955. **Diver Fernando Platas won silver at the 2000 Olympics** and represented Mexico in four consecutive Olympic Games.

956. **Football coach Salvador Reyes** led the Mexican national team to victory in the 1999 FIFA Confederations Cup.

957. **Juan Manuel Márquez, a boxing sensation**, achieved multiple world championships and engaged in thrilling battles with Philippine boxing legend Manny Pacquiao.

958. **Mexico is known for bull riding and bullfighting**. It is one of the few countries that still allow bulls to be fought in the traditional way, where bulls are raised to die by a matador's sword.

959. **Salvador Cabañas, a football forward**, enjoyed success in Mexico and abroad and played a pivotal role in Paraguay's national team.

960. **Middle-distance runner Ana Fidelia Quirot** won numerous medals and set records in international competitions.

961. **Sergio "Checo" Pérez, a Formula 1 driver**, has achieved multiple podium finishes and became the first Mexican to win a Grand Prix race.

962. **Renowned golfer Lorena Ochoa** held the top spot in the Women's World Golf Rankings for over three years.

963. **Fighter Mariana Juárez won multiple world titles in the flyweight division** and was known for her tenacity in the ring.

964. **Judoka Nabor Castillo was the first Mexican to win a medal at a World Judo Grand Prix event.**

965. **Ricardo del Real, a taekwondo athlete**, won the 1997 World Cup Taekwondo Championship.

966. **Marco Antonio Barrera is a retired boxer** who held the world title in three weight classes and who fought some of the great bouts of the early 21st century.

967. **Football goalkeeper José Salvador Carmona** played a key role in Mexico's success in the 1999 FIFA Confederations Cup.

Mexican Actors, Musicians, and Celebrities

In this section, you'll learn about thirty-three of **the most famous Mexican actors, singers, and musicians.** Like the United States, **Mexico is a celebrity culture**, and online papers and social media carry stories about them daily. **Each name on this list represents a story of talent, passion, and dedication**, and their contributions have enriched the artistic landscape of Mexico and beyond. **From award-winning actors and visionary filmmakers to chart-topping musicians and influential artists,** this compilation celebrates the diversity and **creativity that Mexico has brought** to the global stage.

968. **Actor and producer Gael García Bernal** is known throughout the world. He began his career as a child actor and recently co-founded the production company Canana Films.

969. **Director Diego Luna made the critically acclaimed film *Cesar Chavez*,** which is about the struggles of the famous Mexican-American labor leader. Diego Luna is also known for appearing as Cassian Andor in the *Star Wars* universe.

970. **Alfonso Cuarón won two Academy Awards for Best Director for *Gravity*** (2013) and *Roma* (2018).

971. Making hits since the 1960s, **Carlos Santana is known for his signature guitar sound called "Santana sound"** and is in the Rock and Roll Hall of Fame.

972. **Popular singer Thalía is known as the Queen of Latin Pop** and has sold fifty million records worldwide.

973. **Eugenio Derbez is one of Mexico's most successful comedians** and has appeared in several Hollywood films.

974. **Artist and pop culture icon Frida Kahlo** was renowned for her unique self-portraits and is considered one of Mexico's greatest artists.

975. **Alejandro González Iñárritu was the first Mexican filmmaker** to be nominated for an Academy Award as a director and producer. He has also won an Oscar for Best Picture and Best Screenplay.

History of Mexico

976. **Vicente Fernández was a legendary Mexican ranchera singer** and actor known as **El Rey de la Música Ranchera** ("The King of Ranchera Music"). His most famous song is "Guadalajara."

977. **Pedro Infante is considered one of the greatest actors and singers** of the golden age of Mexican cinema (1936–1959).

978. **Singer Luis Miguel is often referred to as El Sol de México** ("The Sun of Mexico") and is one of the most successful Latin American artists of all time. He was born in Puerto Rico but has lived most of his life in Mexico.

979. **Kate del Castillo** gained international attention for her role as **Teresa Mendoza** in the hit **TV series** *La Reina del Sur* (*Queen of the South*).

980. **Ricardo Montalbán played the iconic character Mr. Roarke** in the television series *Fantasy Island*. He also played Khan in *Star Trek II: Wrath of Khan*.

981. **Ana de la Reguera starred in the critically acclaimed film *Nacho Libre* alongside Jack Black.** She has also starred in telenovelas and HBO shows.

982. **Juan Gabriel was a prolific singer-songwriter** and is considered one of the greatest Mexican musicians of all time.

983. **Diego Rivera was an internationally renowned painter** and muralist and was married to Frida Kahlo.

984. **Dolores del Río was one of the first Mexican actresses** to achieve international recognition and success in Hollywood.

985. **Mario Moreno "Cantinflas" was a beloved comedian** and actor known for his quick wit and humorous social commentary.

986. **Carlos Slim is one of the wealthiest individuals in the world** and has made significant philanthropic contributions in Mexico. He owns several businesses, but most of his money comes from telecommunications. He is working to bring Mexican sports to more US television networks.

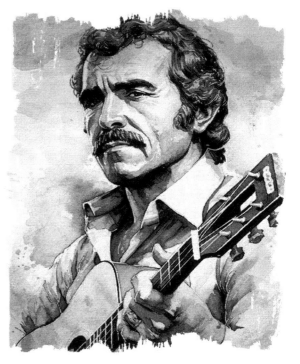

987. **Chavela Vargas was an influential ranchera singer** and a symbol of Mexican LGBTQ+ culture. She was born in Costa Rica but lived in Mexico for over seventy years.

988. **Emilio Azcárraga Jean is the CEO of Grupo Televisa**, one of the largest media companies in the Spanish-speaking world.

989. **Salma Hayek is an international movie star** who got her start in Mexican telenovelas (soap operas).

990. **Julio Iglesias is a renowned singer and songwriter** and is one of the best-selling Latin artists of all time.

991. **Diego Boneta gained international fame for his portrayal of Luis Miguel** in the TV series *Luis Miguel: The Series*.

992. **Belinda began her career as a child actress** and has transitioned into a successful singer and actress.

993. **Paulina Rubio is a pop icon** and has sold over twenty million records worldwide. She is often credited with bringing interest back to Latin music in the 1990s.

994. **Benny Ibarra is a singer, songwriter, and actor** known for his solo career and as a member of the band Timbiriche.

995. **Lucero has been a prominent figure in Mexican entertainment** since childhood and is known for her successful singing and acting career.

996. **Kuno Becker is an actor and singer** who gained popularity for his role as Santiago Muñez in the film *Goal!*

997. **Kalimba is a singer, songwriter**, and actor known for his soulful voice and charismatic performances.

998. **Natalia Lafourcade is a Grammy-winning singer-songwriter** known for her fusion of Latin American folk and pop music.

999. **Grupo Firme is a Mexican musical group** known for their energetic performances and unique blend of regional Mexican music styles. The group was formed in 2013 by their lead vocalist and founder, Eduin Caz, in Tijuana, Baja California, Mexico.

1000. **Guillermo del Toro has won Academy Awards** for Best Picture, Best Director, and Best Animated Feature. He has worked on multiple blockbusters, including **Hellboy** and **Pacific Rim**.

Conclusion

Mexican history is a tapestry woven with ancient civilizations, colonization, revolutions, and cultural richness. **From the pre-Columbian era to the present day, Mexico's history** has shaped its identity as a nation that embraces its **indigenous heritage** while navigating complex challenges and forging its path toward progress.

Today, Mexico is a modern, vibrant country with a much more stable political structure than before. However, it still **struggles with corruption, immigration** issues, and a tremendous amount of **gang violence** caused by the immense profits from the sale and trafficking of illegal drugs. Although it is facing more than its fair share of problems, **people recognize Mexico as a cultural powerhouse.**

Sources and Additional References

Captivating History. *History of Mexico*. 2020.

Jaffary, Nora. *Mexican History: A Primary Source Reader*. 2009.

O'Neill, Bill. *The Great Book of Mexico: Interesting Stories, Mexican History & Random Facts About Mexico*. 2020.

Shawcross, Edward. *The Last Great Emperor of Mexico*. 2021.

Sherman, William. *The Course of Mexican History*. 1979.

Smith, Benjamin. *The Dope: The Real History of the Mexican Drug Trade*. 2021.

Check out another book in the series

Welcome Aboard, Check Out This Limited-Time Free Bonus!

Ahoy, reader! Welcome to the Ahoy Publications family, and thanks for snagging a copy of this book! Since you've chosen to join us on this journey, we'd like to offer you something special.

Check out the link below for a FREE e-book filled with delightful facts about American History.

But that's not all - you'll also have access to our exclusive email list with even more free e-books and insider knowledge. Well, what are ye waiting for? Visit the link below to join and set sail toward exciting adventures in American History.

To access your limited-time free bonus, go to: ahoypublications.com/

Made in the USA
Las Vegas, NV
01 April 2024

88119335R00059